Create Intimacy...
in as little as 8 seconds a day!

Ignite the Passion You Crave

Wayne Ottum and Deborah Kiernan-Ottum

Published by OE Press, a Division of Ottum Enterprises, LLC

Copyright © 2012, 2013 Ottum Enterprises, LLC
218 Main St., #263
Kirkland, WA 98033
www.ottumenterprises.com
info@ottumenterprises.com

Cover design by Lauri Cook, iMarc Consulting, LLC
www.imarcconsulting.com

All Rights Reserved. No part of this book may be reproduced in any form or by any electronic or mechanical means including information storage and retrieval systems without the permission in writing from the publisher, except by a reviewer, who may quote a brief passage in their review. First paperback edition, 2012.

ISBN-13: 978-0615468075

ISBN-10: 0615468071

LIBRARY OF CONGRESS CONTROL NUMBER: 2012916115

Contents

Foreword 1
Notes of Appreciation 7
Introduction 9
    Our Message to Women 10
    Our Message to Men 12
    Our Message to Both of You 15
    Meet Our Example Couples 16
Intimacy as the Foundation of Your Relationship 21
    The Passion Pyramid 23
    Any Time, Any Where 25
    The Intimate Moment Cycle™ 27
    Making the Intimate Moment Cycle™ Work for You ... 32
Making Intimacy Work for You 39
    We Have Different Views 40
    Men and Women are Inherently Different 53
    We Communicate Differently 57
    We Are Motivated Differently 71
    As We Grow, We Change 89
From Theory to Practice 95
    Touch 99
    Taste 102
    Smell 106
    A Few Little Words 108
    The Kiss 113

From a Distance	115
Something For Him	117
Something For Her	119
Around the House	120
In The Bedroom	122
Out and About	124
Just Between the Two of Us!	128
With Others	131
The Little Things	132
Putting it All Together	**137**
An Introduction to Passionate Pursuits™	141
In Closing	152
About the Authors	**153**

Foreword

by haleyheart keepers*

Tree of Life Celebration

I believe that Wayne Ottum and Deborah Kiernan-Ottum's work, which is exemplified in this ground breaking book, *Create Intimacy... in as little as 8 seconds a day*, addresses areas that need attention on a global scale. These same areas are the foundation of the consciousness the community members of Tree of Life Celebration (www.treeoflifecelebration.com) believe in so deeply -- the need to create and continually shepherd healthy, consciously-intentioned relationships. At the heart of our mission and purpose we see the need for humanity to become aware, for every person step up, take back their personal power, be accountable for self, and honor their commitment to authenticity and personal integrity. With each individual who chooses to be a whole, healthy, non-ego-centered person, the benefit grows for everyone. This is at the heart of our connection. I see Wayne and Deborah's work being very pivotal and foundational in applying these concepts in another level and manner – the one-to-one relationships that are often ignored, misunderstood, assumed to be "just fine" or simply disregarded.

These are not just the relationships of committed couples, but also the parent-child, the friend-friend, the sibling-sibling, co-workers, colleagues and more. Today, life itself is a collection of relationship groups interacting in a rapidly devolving structure of values, socio-economic and political conditions, all inside a framework of rapid change. When the foundation is not solid (such as the couple, family, social circle, community of friends, etc.), how can the larger structures (work environments, business/client relationships, governance groups, etc.) be healthy and functional?

The only other person I've examined at a deeper level that has attempted something of this magnitude is Greg Baer (*Real Love,* and all the other books that take his principal theory and apply it to *Real Love in Family Relationship, in Marriage, in Business,* etc.). Though powerful on its own, Baer's work is more conceptual, where I find Wayne and Deborah's work emphasizes more of the "practical and tactical" elements that are often so needed for humans desiring to change their behaviors. This is especially true for those new to the ideas. The Ottums are *way-showers* with specifics that anyone can understand and apply as they start, modify or tune-up their journey of creating, building and maintaining healthy, inspiring relationships.

Wayne and Deborah's material is relevant for people of all ages, but so critically important for the younger generations – many of whom have never witnessed a healthy, functional relationship. It seems our young people have the heart and understanding that love gets more than hate, most of the time; however, many in this generation have rejected old paradigms and because they don't yet know what will work, they live less than fully as they meet their own challenges and struggles through trial and error. Some emulate bits and pieces of advice from friends or parents, with no real understanding of the larger fabric of successful relationships.

I have the privilege of knowing the Ottums personally. Their own stories and life experience brought them together, to do this important work as partners. Both are accomplished individuals in their own right… Both are living what they teach in their own relationship, the way they've brought their families together, the way they approach life and love, and in the work they are doing with their clientele. Both are thoughtful, mindful, heart-inspired people who have stepped up and stepped out to make the world a better place, one relationship at a time.

Most would agree, the world we live in today has become short-term sighted, consumeristic and disposable. It's not a surprise that we have so many large issues that reflect back to the most essential foundations. These are the foundations of love and family. Huge divorce rates, single parent families, latch-key kids – each of these create and deliver damaged goods into an environment that, not surprisingly, produces individuals who are less than whole. Some arrive with incredulity in the belief that something magical will simply happen – that they will have what they want, live healthy lives, have meaningful work relationships, a strong sense of community - all with ZERO effort. Like my favorite quote from Dr. Phil McGraw, it would be at this point where he asks, "So how's that working for you?" Clearly it isn't.

Tree of Life Celebration is heading in the direction of helping many move to conscious, intention-based living as individuals first and then with an eye toward "the Best and Highest Good Outcomes for All Parties Involved." The Ottum's are "working at the coal-seam interface" of this transformation change by helping people, aware and unaware, who may or may not realize exactly why they are where they are. People who just want their life to be different and better... Those who desire a deeper, more meaningful, more intimate, relationship. The Ottums offer concrete, proven ideas and support to create a plan of action, carry it out, and make the shift. I would recommend that everyone read this book.

haleyheart keepers* co-creator of *Tree of Life Celebration*

About Tree of Life Celebration

The Tree of Life symbolically illustrates that all life is connected. The Tree of Life concept permeates the human collective experience, as exhibited globally throughout science, religion, philosophy and mythology. We embrace this idea of Tree of Life Celebration(s) as a starting point for unity from which we intend to branch out. We believe that unity is a co-creative process and encourage all to contribute to the process of anchoring the unity consciousness on the planet through their heart, actions and talents. Visit www.treeoflifecelebration.com for more information.

In keeping with the intention of a new way of being that is non-ego centric and collaboratively created, the co-creators of Tree of Life Celebration chose to adopt pen names in their interactions with all who are part of the community.

Notes of Appreciation

There are so many people to thank for helping us bring this book to you.

To our children Tessa, Jesse, Adrienne, Zac and Mack, thank you for believing in us, and for your love and support.

To our many friends who have encouraged us to put our ideas into the written word, we thank you!

Thank you to Lauri Cook of iMarc Consulting, LLC., the talent behind our branding and marketing and the gifted designer of our book covers.

Thank you to our reviewers, Connie Tomlinson, Marie Maguire, Cindy Carlton and Yvonne Salinas. We could not have done this without you!

Thank you to our many clients who continue to inspire us. It is the success you have achieved that gives us the continued motivation to provide our services and find new and innovative ways to share our ideas.

And thanks to you for choosing this book from the many relationship books out there. It is our commitment to you to challenge you to define and live, with purpose and intent, the relationship of your dreams. We trust you will find this book to be a valuable and useful tool in your journey together.

Introduction

> *"It is not time or opportunity that is to determine **intimacy**; it is disposition alone. Seven years would be insufficient to make some people acquainted with each other, and seven days are more than enough for others."*
> Jane Austin

Imagine yourself at a party with a mixture of friends, new and old, male and female. During a lively conversation over dinner, the topic of *intimacy* is brought up. Most of the women in the group will lean in a little closer, and their immediate and full attention is evident. It's obvious they want to hear more. A few women, however, may look skeptical and think, "What intimacy?" knowing that finding it is a lot harder than simply desiring it.

In sharp contrast, however, several of the men in this group will either pretend not to have heard and may look terribly uncomfortable if you pursue their participation. Some may come up with a couple of crass jokes or disconnect from the conversation. One or two may even look around frantically for somewhere to run, or a few might be intrigued, thinking the conversation has just turned to *sex*, and now, they're all ears!

The point we are trying to make with this little vignette is that *intimacy* has vastly different meanings to men and women, and more to the point, to each of us, as individuals. In general, however, women love to talk about intimacy, and they want more of it in their relationship; and in general, most men think intimacy is code for sex, or fear discussing it because it means they have to vocalize and share their feelings.

Regardless of how you might react to the subject of intimacy, we have a candid and straightforward message for you. It is a message that challenges conventional wisdom. It is, we believe, a message that encourages you to think differently, more positively and more proactively about how to create and enhance intimacy, romance and passion in your relationship.

Our Message to Women

If you are a woman, we might have had you with the photo on the cover and the title! You likely picked up the book because you desire more intimacy, romance, and passion with your partner. You would like to discuss your feelings on these topics openly, and you want that discussion to lead to action (in more ways than one). Or, you may simply want the spark back in your relationship that you experienced in your early years together, and you have been looking for new ways to make that happen. If so, this is the right book to help you get there.

If you are a woman who believes it is your partner's responsibility to keep the romance alive in your relationship, you have also found the right book. You may be looking for ways to encourage your partner to be more romantic, (i.e., send flowers, buy gifts, plan dates, and woo you again like they did in the beginning). You may have picked up this book as "a gift" for them to read in hopes they might take the hint. Yes, this book touts a promise that it only takes 8 seconds to create intimacy, and you may be hopeful your partner can put forth that much effort. Yes, it is true that it only takes seconds to create an intimate moment and your partner, no matter their gender, can handle it. We all can!

If you want more intimacy, romance and passion in your relationship, it's important to remember that the first place to look is in the mirror. You can get more of what you want in your relationship by giving your partner more of what they need (and the same is true for them).

The most basic premise of this book is that as a committed couple, each partner is *equally* responsible for the amount of, or lack of, intimacy, romance and passion in your relationship. If you desire to have a deeper, more meaningful connection with your partner, if you want more intimate moments, more romance and more passion, the first place to look is within yourself. It's time to focus on the positive and take an equal share of the responsibility for the current state of your relationship, good, bad or in between. We show you how, one step at a time.

This book will challenge you to look deep within and be honest with yourself, perhaps for the first time, about your needs and your role in your relationship. With honest exploration and communication, you WILL get more of what you want, and your partner will get more of what they need.

Our Message to Men

Guys, let's talk frankly… You may have picked up this book hoping it might help you get more of what you want from your relationship (i.e., more sex), thinking that if you only have to focus 8 seconds a day to build a stronger connection with your partner, that you could probably handle that, right?

Or, if your partner just handed this book to you and proclaimed, "Look what I just got us, honey," take a deep breath and relax. We want you to know this book has been written with you in mind as well. This is **not** another book about how all men are Neanderthals and you need to change every aspect of who you are. We wrote this book for BOTH men and women and we made sure all points of view are represented in a way that respects your intelligence and your unique needs. (And, by the way, there is nothing wrong with wanting more sex. More on that later...)

But let's also be clear guys, if you are not getting enough of what you want in your relationship, the FIRST place to look is in the mirror. So if you do consider yourself a Neanderthal and think a relationship consists of dragging your woman back to the cave for her to do your bidding, this book is DEFINITELY for you. We hope to show you, however, a more positive and effective way to get more of what you want in your relationship.

The basic premise of this book is: *To get more of what you want in your relationship, whatever that is, the secret is giving your partner more of what they need!* It is that simple, and yet it is still a challenge.

It's simple, because it works! Just like a beautiful green lawn, it is all about creating and lovingly caring for the foundation on which it stands - the soil. If you want a great lawn, you wouldn't just scatter dirt and seed, pray for rain, hope for the best, and leave it alone to take care of itself. But, in general, that is what we, as men, tend to do with our relationships. We "acquire" our partner and then we check off that box and move on to the next thing to conquer. But if you want to have that amazing lawn, year after year, you care for it. You feed it, water it, weed it, edge it, and mow it. So ask yourself now, how much care and feeding have you given your relationship lately? Have you tilled and conditioned the soil and kept it watered? Have you done anything about the weeds that have sprung up?

As we mentioned earlier, this may also be a *challenging* process because it requires you to think and **talk** about what you need. It means taking the time to understand your desires and then putting your thoughts into words, on paper. It requires both of you to be clear about your needs, to be vulnerable and talk about these things openly with your partner, and to actively listen to their needs as well. That is not always easy. As men, we tend to avoid those *"honey, we need to talk"* moments. In fact, this step may be your biggest challenge; and we help you through it, in a way that works best for you.

If you desire more of what you want in your relationship, regardless of whether that is more sex, more understanding, more appreciation, more cave time, more intimacy (as you define it), or all of the above, AND you are open to making the commitment to "till the soil," so to speak, then read on. Our commitment to you is that we will provide you with simple concepts and easily executable ideas in a way that makes sense to you. We promise you WILL get more of what you want – and so will your partner!

Our Message to Both of You

This book is for committed couples who desire more intimacy in their relationship, regardless of age or sexual orientation, or how many years they have been together. The *definition* of intimacy is up to you, as individuals, and together as a couple. Regardless of the male and female stereotypes or how society or anyone else may define intimacy, YOU get to choose what intimacy means to you and how to use that definition to get more of IT in your relationship. There are no right answers, only the answers that are right for you, your partner, and your relationship. Period.

We challenge you to read this book together with an open mind to one simple idea, that you are both equally responsible for the current state of your relationship, for good or for bad. Commit to grow together throughout this process and you will find significant value in this book and develop the confidence to create the relationship of your dreams.

We challenge you to go through each process without pre-conceived notions of what you think your own or your partner's answers "should" be. Be respectful of and open to accepting the results for yourself and your partner as they are made clear to you. Having an open mind to the process of self-discovery allows you to truly explore the concepts and develop answers that are true and authentic to you, not what society or your partner, or anyone else may expect. Being truly accepting of whatever your partner may decide for themselves frees them to explore their needs so they can communicate them to you honestly and openly without fear of judgment. The most loving thing you can do for yourself and your partner is to accept and respect whatever is discovered throughout this process.

If you want a better, deeper, more meaningful, life-long relationship filled with intimacy, romance and passion, then you're in the right place. By the time you are done reading this book and completing the exercises, you will be practicing a very simple process that makes sense and you will be experiencing more intimacy in your relationship. You will be implementing new ideas into your relationship that you can tailor to meet your needs as a couple, and **you will be building the life-long connection you desire together.**

Meet Our Example Couples

To help you relate to the concepts and tools in this book to your own life and relationship, we would like to introduce you to four couples. Each couple is in a different stage of life and their relationship, and all are committed to each other. They share the same desire for more intimacy in their relationship, however, they all have very different definitions of what intimacy means to them.

Couple #1: Recently Married

Ron and Susan are recently married. They still have that fresh, new and exciting feel to their relationship and they are very, VERY much in love with each other. They have heard the marriage horror stories from well meaning family and friends as well as all the jokes about how the honeymoon won't last forever. Neither of them wants their relationship to end in divorce, like their parents' marriages did. Or end up like their friends, Pete and Joan. Pete says things to Ron like, *"You know... after 7 years, the passion's all gone, buddy. I guess I don't need to worry about that flower and candy crap anymore. She doesn't appreciate it anyway."* And Joan confides in Susan and says things like, *"I'd love to be more intimate with Pete, but I just don't feel the connection anymore. It's like I'm not even there and the football game or his computer are more important than me, and that really hurts."* Ron and Susan are concerned for their friends and believe it doesn't have to be that way. They are on a quest to discover how to stay connected in their relationship through every stage of their lives together, and they believe through the eyes of young love, that they will beat the odds and live happily ever after.

Couple #2: Together 5 Years

Chris and John have been living together for 5 years. They have great chemistry and love each other deeply. Both of them independently, however, have confided in friends that their relationship has gotten a little predictable. There is still great attraction and positive energy in their relationship; however, it seems to Chris that John doesn't really understand what he needs. Chris isn't sure how John feels about him or their relationship because John never talks about it. To Chris, everything feels like it's all about John all the time whenever they go out. John, on the other hand, thinks he's planning things that Chris will find fun and romantic. John also feels that Chris doesn't know what he (John) needs. John hears Chris when he talks about needing more intimacy and romance in their relationship, so John continues to make an effort by planning more things to do together, however, what he does for Chris never seems to be appreciated. At times, his efforts are not even acknowledged and that hurt's John's feelings. Both of them are discouraged and their relationship is beginning to break down.

Couple #3: Married with Children

Bob and Sarah have been married 10 years. They have 2 beautiful children, successful careers, a lovely home in a great neighborhood and relatively new cars. They are very active together in the community, and work hard at raising their family. Bob and Sarah love each other, and they love their kids. Over the years, however, their lives have become ridiculously busy yet very routine. Yes, there is comfort in routine, but the routine they've fallen into is not meeting their personal needs or their needs as a couple. Each feels disconnected, but they don't really understand how that happened or why; nor do they know how to discuss it, and they tend to get irritated with each other now over little things that really don't matter. They want the intimacy, romance and passion in their relationship again but they don't know where to begin to get it back.

Couple #4: Soon to be Empty Nesters

José and Carmen have just celebrated their 25th wedding anniversary. They were married young, raised 3 healthy kids, and are now facing the next stage of their life as empty nesters. Their youngest son will be going off to college in a few months. Their daughter is expecting and they are excited to be grandparents for the first time very soon. José owns a business that has provided for them nicely over the years; and Carmen has been, for the most part, a stay at home mom, or what she likes to call a *"domestic engineer... the hardest job in the world!"* José agrees with her and has admired her strength and courage through some particularly difficult times over the years with the kids. They knew this time was coming, alone time together without kids, but they feel unprepared now and apprehensive, especially as José considers retirement in the next few years. Their deep love for each other is still there, but it lacks the spark they had before and hoped to have at this time in their lives. They feel like they are different people than the two kids they were when they married, and now they realize they still have half their lives left to live - together. They long for the passion they once shared before work, kids, and other obligations dampened the fire. Now that they have the time to focus on themselves and each other, they don't know how to reignite that connection and they're beginning to wonder if it's too late for them to find it again.

Do one of these couples remind you of your relationship with your partner? Whatever your situation, whether together for 1 year, 5, 10, 25, or more, whether you're young or old, gay or straight, with a house full of children or none at all, or you just shipped your last kid off to college and don't know what to do with yourself or each other now, this little book can help you. It can help you discover how to keep intimacy alive, enhance the intimacy you have, or find what you've misplaced along the way… *It will help you find that spark that reignites the fire (connection) in your relationship.*

It's time to introduce you to a simple process that you can use at any time to discover, enhance, and maintain the intimacy in your relationship; a process that can take as little as 8 seconds. Everyone has 8 seconds to give, especially when the reward for giving more of what your partner needs is receiving more of what you want, which in turn, strengthens your relationship as a whole and creates the foundation for a lifetime of romance and passion with the one you love.

Intimacy as the Foundation of Your Relationship

"When love is accompanied with deep intimacy, it raises us to the highest level of human experience."
Leo Buscaglia – Born For Love

First things first, what IS intimacy?

According to Webster's dictionary, ***intimacy*** is defined as, *"the state of being intimate; belonging to or characterizing one's deepest nature; marked by very close association, contact, or familiarity; a warm friendship developing through long association suggesting informal warmth or privacy; and something of a very personal or private nature."*

Honestly, it doesn't matter what the dictionary has to say about intimacy; **what really matters is what intimacy means to you and your partner!** In our experience, we found most couples have never really talked about this, let alone thought much about it themselves. It is time to better understand yourself and your partner in that regard, and this little book will help you do just that. Knowledge is power and understanding your needs and the needs of your partner is the key to getting more of the intimacy you both crave.

It is of utmost importance to understand each other's "idea" of intimacy so you can use that information to direct and focus your communication during the snippets of time you do have each day to connect with your partner – so you can communicate and create intimacy in a way they understand.

As we mentioned before, the secret of getting more of what you want is *giving* more of what your partner needs. Do you want more intimacy? Then give more, but communicated in a way that is understood by your partner. Do you want more romance and passion? Give more romance in the way your partner understands, and the passion you desire will follow! It's really that simple.

And it doesn't have to be constant. No relationship can sustain 24/7 wooing, champagne, chocolate and roses, especially as that relationship grows and matures over time. It is possible, however, to continually discover, enhance, regain and maintain intimacy, romance, and passion in your relationship, AND increase the temperature of each to keep the home fires burning for a lifetime. The key, once again, is the continual communication and adaptation to your own and your partner's needs.

That's why we believe *intimacy* (as defined by you and your partner) is the foundation of a loving relationship on which romance and passion are built and sustained, as well as the engine that drives the romantic energy in the relationship. Intimacy is about the connection, direct communication, understanding, trust that comes from close association, contact and familiarity, and very personal and private interactions between two people. Being intimate says, "I love you," and so much more!

The Passion Pyramid

Intimacy is the foundation of every loving, healthy relationship and intimate moments can happen, literally, anywhere and at any moment. Romantic moments, on the other hand, build from that foundation of intimacy and often take planning. It is the planning and effort that, in large part, makes those moments even more special. And without the energy intimacy creates, the desire for romance wanes. If the energy is there, romantic moments will occur naturally and can be more deeply experienced. Then comes passion, that deep physical and emotional drive (attraction) or feeling (expression) for one another. True passion can rarely be achieved when one or both partners do not feel intimately connected, understood, and trusted. And it is often the romantic gestures that fan the embers created by intimacy to stoke the fire so passion can be released.

The close relationship between intimacy, romance, and passion is described here in what we call "The Passion Pyramid".

Figure 1: The Passion Pyramid

Though romantic gestures and deep passionate moments may not happen every day, you can always, at any moment, experience *intimacy*. Intimate moments are the glue that binds a relationship and keeps the loving energy alive between the big, special, romantic interludes that lead to passionate adventures. And with a solid feeling (foundation) of continued intimacy supporting and leading to romantic moments, couples can experience the passion they desire, creating memories that will keep them connected for a lifetime.

When intimacy is not present, however, trust and communication breaks down and the energy of the relationship begins to decrease. Sadly, the desire for romance deteriorates, and romantic moments become fewer and farther between. In turn, there is less opportunity created for passion to be released. And when one or both in the relationship feels a lack of romance and passion, and their needs continue to go unmet, the relationship begins to fail seriously and one of three things will happen:

- Couples will remain in a very unhappy and unhealthy relationship with resentment and angst; or
- Intimacy, romance, and passion will be sought out elsewhere with someone else; or
- Divorce is eminent. You can almost feel this inevitability for Pete and Joan, the friends of our young couple, Ron and Susan, who are on their way to giving up on regaining any intimacy in their relationship.

Any Time, Any Where

It comes down to a focus on *intimacy*. What is wonderful and empowering is realizing that intimate moments can happen at any time in your relationship. They can happen first thing after waking in the morning, while eating breakfast, during the work day, over dinner, while reading or watching television together, and certainly at bedtime. Intimate moments don't need to be planned or managed. They can be spontaneous, spur of the moment, and on a whim.

Intimate moments can also happen anywhere: at home, in the car, at work, while out to dinner alone together or with friends, on vacation, or even while waiting in line together at the grocery store checkout. They can happen in any room in the house: the kitchen, living room and, of course, the bedroom.

Intimate moments can be in many forms. They can be spoken or not involve a single word. They can be a gesture, a sticky note, a text message, a private tweet, or a gift. They can be a touch of the hand, a kiss, or a knowing glance. Intimate moments can even happen when you are apart.

If you desire to create a more solid foundation of intimacy in your relationship, the important thing to remember is… ***Intimate moments require the desire and intent of both partners to create them, every chance you get.*** Each partner must recognize the opportunity to create an intimate moment, and then take action with a gesture, a loving word, etc. And then, it is equally important for the other to recognize the intent, make the connection in the moment, and respond with appreciation.

Imagine the power that can be generated when both of you are committed to making intimate moments together! But even if one of the two doesn't completely buy into "creating" these moments in your day-to-day, this energy is so powerful that one of you could initiate intimate gestures in a way that is understood by your partner and, with patience and understanding, the messages will eventually be received and acknowledged. It may likely be hit-or-miss at first, and perhaps a bit frustrating, but eventually the other will warm up to the loving attention and the Intimate Moment Cycle™ will be completed.

Regardless, your efforts will create more intimate moment opportunities in your relationship, which is always a good thing!

The Intimate Moment Cycle™

Intimate moments, when fully realized, go through what we call the **Intimate Moment Cycle**™ (see **Figure 2** on page 28). This cycle depicts how a simple gesture can become a deep, meaningful, and emotional moment that adds to and strengthens the foundation of your relationship and fuels the love you have for each other. This process of real, meaningful, relationship-building moments can happen

> **HINT:** You can use this cycle to improve any relationship, parent-child, friend-friend, etc.

in as little as 8 seconds. Seriously! You CAN build positive power and loving energy in your relationship in as little as 8 seconds a day; and we challenge you to give it a try for yourself in your relationship.

Remember, any intimate moment begins with a gesture. It can be a word, a touch, or an action. But that gesture is only the beginning. To truly connect and make it a meaningful moment, the receiver must go through the following five-step process:

1. **RECOGNIZE:** As the receiver of the gesture you need to be able to recognize it for what it is; an opportunity to connect, an opportunity for intimacy.

2. **BE PRESENT:** When you recognize the intimate gesture, you need to stop, disconnect from what you are doing or thinking, and be PRESENT in that moment.

3. **CONNECT:** With eye contact, a touch, or body language, make a connection with your partner to demonstrate you are ready to receive the message.

4. **LISTEN:** Tune in and "listen" with your heart and all your senses to truly hear, feel and accept the message.

5. **RESPOND:** Once the message has been received, then it is your turn to respond and show your partner that you have received the message and express your gratitude for the gesture and the opportunity to connect.

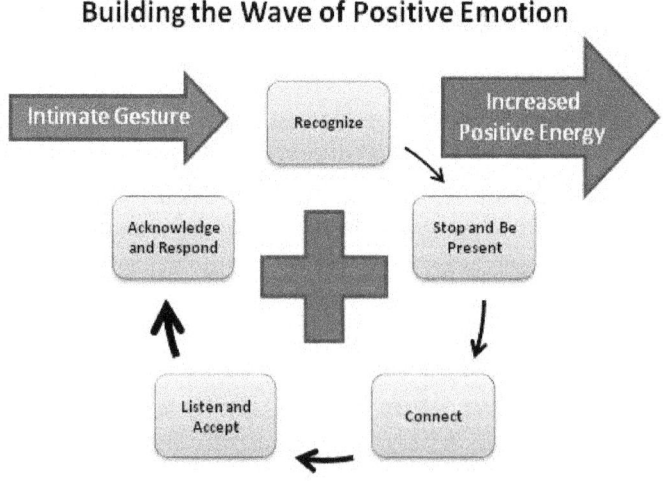

Figure 2: The Intimate Moment Cycle™

Like powerful ocean waves, continued completion of the Intimate Moment Cycle™ builds positive flow (energy) and increases the size of the positive emotional wave.

Sadly, the opposite is also true. The *Negative Emotion Cycle* (see **Figure 3** below) shows us that whenever an intimate moment opportunity is missed, the loving energy of the relationship may be depleted. Whenever an intimate moment is not recognized and the Intimate Moment Cycle™ is not completed, frustration, anger, and resentment may build, creating negative energy pushing back against the desire for intimacy.

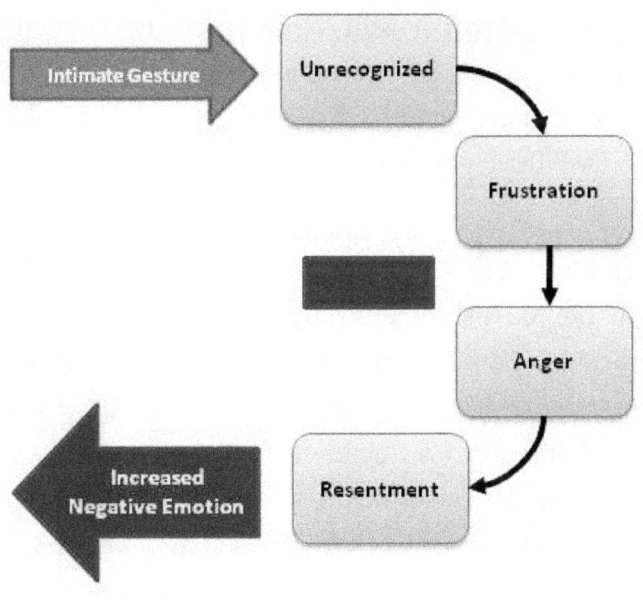

Figure 3: The Negative Emotion Cycle

Do you remember how you felt the last time you tried to connect with your partner and they didn't even acknowledge the effort, or they were too distracted to respond?

As an example, when did it become OK to read/respond to a text message in the middle of a conversation with your loved one? Smart phones can be a powerful tool when we manage them to stay connected with family, friends, our jobs; sadly for many, however, cell phones have become the Master and we react instantly (like Pavlov's dogs) when the bell rings. Although some may believe times have changed with the onslaught of virtual connectivity, in reality, it is *still* rude when someone interrupts a conversation whether in person, or virtually, and ruder still to allow it to happen and continue. What this conditioned response tells your partner is quite clear, "This person (or thing) is more important than you are to me right now." In a word, OUCH!

Think about what it feels like when you're ignored. It might not be the other's intention, but when they are distracted and disconnected while you're trying to communicate and connect with them, the message received in return is "ignored." CA-CHING! A hefty withdrawal was just taken out of your love account. According to the work of Willard F. Harley, Jr., Ph.D. who is best known for his internationally bestselling book, *His Needs, Her Needs: Building An Affair-Proof Marriage*, like a bank account, if there hasn't been enough "love deposits" to off-set the withdrawal, your love account becomes overdrawn and resentment may set in. Definitely NOT the result either of you were hoping for.

Therefore, not only can the Intimate Moment Cycle™ create an intimate moment out of an ordinary one, completing the cycle will build positive emotional energy that drives your relationship forward (increasing the positive balance in your love account) **and** will eliminate the potential negative emotional energy that can sabotage your intent and desire (decreasing the number of withdrawals). Completing the cycle is the key to building the emotional energy for romance which, in turn, increases the energy of the wave so passion can be experienced in a way that is most meaningful to your relationship.

It really can be as simple as tuning into each other for as little as 8 seconds! Paying attention to the daily opportunities for intimacy that arise in your life together and completing the five steps of the Intimate Moment Cycle™ will help you experience more intimate moments in your relationship and set the stage for improved and increased romance and passion.

Now you can understand the importance of developing good communication and truly understanding your partner's definition of intimacy. If you want more in your relationship, the key is giving your partner more of what they need - *in the way they need it.*

The result, in what begins with as little as 8 seconds a day, will be a stronger foundation and plenty of fuel for the fires of romance and passion in your relationship, no matter your age or how long you have been together.

Making the Intimate Moment Cycle™ Work for You

Let's take a closer look at the Intimate Moment Cycle™ and how it can work for you, step by step.

Recognizing an Intimate Moment

Recognizing the intimate moment – *in that moment* – is probably the most difficult of the five steps, especially if you have been disconnected from your partner for some time. **It's simple**, but takes practice. In the beginning, you will likely miss a few opportunities as you break old habits. No worries! You simply recognize that you missed one and act intentionally to create another.

To assist you in better recognizing an intimate moment, we provide 104 tried-and-true intimate suggestions later in this book (starting on page 95). Review these ideas with your partner and discuss which ones appeal to you most individually and as a couple. Talk about how to make them more recognizable for each other. Have fun with this! You can even use our suggestions as examples and come up with your own ideas. Keep an open mind as you begin, and be patient. If your partner misses an intimate moment, be kind, and simply say, *"Intimate moment here."* Or, *"Intimate moment, next left!"* Make a joke and laugh about it together to lighten the mood. The important thing is to enter into this experience with the assumption that you both want to be, and intend to be more intimate with each other. Move forward lovingly, and resolve to laugh *A LOT* during the process.

In our own relationship, it helped us to borrow an expression from the movie, *Avatar*, that acts as a prompt (a reminder) for us to center ourselves and it grounds us in a split second to pay attention and recognize the opportunity to create an intimate moment. For those of you who have not seen *Avatar*, the term, *"I see you,"* goes beyond the simple literal expression. It's much deeper, more like, *"I see all that you are, body, soul, and spirit."* When one of us says, *"I see you,"* to the other, we become IMMEDIATELY present, our eyes lock on each other's, and we focus with intent. There is an *energy* in this moment that is shared, and a soul connection made so deep that the warmth of it stays with us the entire day. THAT is what keeps love alive. It's THAT connection that keeps you coming back for more – you're home wherever you are, you're safe, you're loved, no question. And you can experience these moments as often as you create them. Take a moment now to look into each other's eyes. You can even come up with your own "prompt" (such as, *"I see you,"* from *Avatar*, or Joey's *"Hello there,"* from *Friends*) to trigger an intimate moment of your own at any time throughout your day.

Being Present

This step is about disconnecting from where you are (in your head or otherwise) and making a conscious choice to be truly present in the moment with your significant other. You may be watching TV together, or doing the dishes, or a number of other things and your partner leans in for a kiss. An opportunity is knocking! Being present in this moment means turning your attention away from what you are doing for a few seconds and making the effort to share that moment with your partner as if the show or chore didn't exist. It is now, in this moment, just the two of you. No TV, no work, no kids, no distractions – for 8 seconds. You can do that!

When you are deep in thought, busy with a chore or a bit stressed out, it may feel annoying at first to be "interrupted," to take your mind off what you are doing in order to "be present" in that moment with your partner to make it intimate. But when you realize the moment is so fleeting, and the cycle so short, and the value added so great, it really only comes down to a few seconds of your time – **it's totally worth it!** The very act of being present in that moment MAKES an intimate moment what it is. Priceless!

Making the Connection

This step is about connecting with your partner so they know you are ready to receive their loving message. It involves facing your partner, making eye contact, touching them, or any other body language that communicates you are present and connected with them, that you understand they are expressing intimacy, and that you are ready to receive their message. When you are not in close proximity to one another, such as responding to a text or private tweet from your partner, the power of being present and connecting is no less important as it is when you are together. Whenever you recognize the intimate opportunity, break away as soon as you are able, tune into the message, and truly connect with your partner as if they were right next to you. Imagine the power of this simple step. Think about the opposite for a moment and remember how you feel when you know someone isn't tuned into you; and the difference in how you feel when you know they are!

Listen and "Hear" the Message

This step is about opening yourself up to "hearing" what your partner is communicating to you through their intimate gesture, whether it is a look, a touch, or a word. At the very least, your partner is reaching out to you and letting you know they wish to connect with you. But there is likely more. When your partner takes your hand as you walk together, they may just want to feel closer to you, or show you that you're on their mind, or that they love and appreciate you, or all of the above! Each intimate gesture has a meaning behind it beyond the obvious and when you take that moment to really listen with your soul, you will "hear" it, even in the touch of a hand, a passing glance or a private tweet. And if you are still not sure, just ASK! There is no harm in that, and you have only a deeper understanding to gain.

Respond

The response to an intimate gesture can be as simple as a smile, a wink, a certain look, a loving word, or a simple emoticon response in a text message. You do not have to *reciprocate* in kind, but to **complete** the cycle – you do need to respond and show your appreciation.

As an example, when your partner rubs your back, you do not have to rub theirs in return. You could – but that's not the point. The intimate gesture is a "gift." Responding with words like, *"that feels good,"* or *"I love your touch,"* or a simple *"thank you,"* tells them you are present in the moment, that you have accepted and acknowledged the gift, and you are thankful for it. The point is to make your partner aware that you noticed. It is giving them the feedback that their intimate gesture was recognized, accepted, and that you "heard them" which is lovingly validating. And remember, it goes both ways. Remember, *"thank you"* are two of the most powerful words in our language. Simply verbalizing or responding in some way with your appreciation for their effort and desire creates powerful, positive emotional energy and fuels the engine of your relationship.

The Intimate Moment Cycle™ is your guide for taking an everyday moment and making it an intimate one. By taking that brief moment to recognize the opportunity, then allowing yourself to be present in it, accepting, acknowledging, and appreciating the simple gesture from your partner, intimacy can be created; and your relationship will become deeper and more meaningful with every passing day.

Making Intimacy Work for You

> *"True intimacy is a human constant.*
> *People of all types find it equally hard to achieve,*
> *equally precious to hold.*
> *Age, education, social status, make little difference here;*
> *even genius does not presuppose the talent to reveal*
> *one's self completely*
> *and completely absorb one's self in another personality.*
> *Intimacy is to love what concentration is to work:*
> *a simultaneous drawing together*
> *to attention and release of energy."*
> Robert Grudin, *Time and the Art of Living*

As our four example couples show you, there are a number of factors involved in keeping intimacy alive and well in a relationship. It is never just *one thing*.

We believe there are five major factors that you need to be aware of:

- People, regardless of their gender, have a different view of, definition of, and need for - ***intimacy***.

- Men and women are inherently different.

- People learn and communicate differently and, therefore, need to be communicated *to* in a way that makes sense to them.
- We are all motivated to act in differing ways.
- Our needs and desires change and grow as we do, over time.

Let's look a little more closely at each of these factors.

We Have Different Views

As individuals, regardless of our gender, our view of intimacy is likely different than our partner's. As our example Couple #3 shows, Bob and Sarah definitely have different viewpoints on intimacy, leading to a disconnect in their relationship, yet neither understands why. Let's see if we can figure it out…

Bob washes Sarah's car inside and out every other Saturday morning, without fail. The opposite Saturday mornings, he loads up the trash and recycle bins and takes them to the transfer station. On his way home, Bob stops at the coffee shop to pick-up Sarah's favorite latte. He also keeps their lawn impeccable, and fixes all the little things around the house because he knows how important it is to Sarah that things look nice and are well taken care of. He's bummed because Sarah doesn't seem to notice these things that he does for her to show her how much he loves her, and how much he does to take care of her and the kids.

Bob feels like he rarely gets a sincere thank you and that would mean so much to him. He would also love it if Sarah did things for him.

Sarah, on the other hand, is always giving Bob hugs and kisses, scratching his back, and massaging his neck. Whenever she walks by, she reaches out and touches him. Even when they are in the car, she likes to have a hand on his leg while he drives. Sarah also tells Bob every day that she loves him. She's upset because she doesn't think Bob appreciates or reciprocates her affections. She longs for Bob to reach out and touch her and say, *"I love you,"* more often.

The truth is BOTH are showing affection (intimacy) in a way that makes sense to them, but not in a way that makes sense to their partner! Most people tend to treat each other in the way they want to be treated. The same holds true here. Bob would likely "get it" if Sarah also did things FOR him to **show** her affection rather than just TO him, and Sarah would drink in every drop of attention if Bob tuned in, touched her more often, and vocalized his love for her in addition to what he is DOING for her.

Bob is a "do-er/pleaser." He equates intimacy with doing things for someone and having things done for him. He does things for Sarah (through action) to make her happy and to show his affection while believing he is being intimate by those actions. These things are important to him and he desires them in return.

Sarah, on the other hand, is a "touchy-feely." She equates spoken words of affirmation and affection with intimacy. It is important to her to connect with Bob (through touch) and to affirm her feelings for him in words, and she desires the same in return from him.

Much has been written to help you understand yourself, your mate and your differences, from Gary Chapman's, *Five Love Languages*, to Dr. John Grey's *Men Are From Mars, Women Are From Venus*, to Willard F. Harley, Jr., Ph.D., *His Needs, Her Needs: Building An Affair-Proof Marriage* mentioned earlier in this book, and everything in between. All provide new insights and thoughts to consider, and we encourage you to continue your quest for more knowledge and understanding through reading, discussions, retreats and seminars. But the bottom line always comes down to answering the following questions honestly and understanding your answers...

What does intimacy mean to you? What does intimacy mean to your partner? It doesn't matter what any author has to say about it, including us! The most important thing to KNOW is what you believe and what your partner believes. If you're like most couples, you haven't thought about it in this context. You might think intimacy means *touching* or *talking,* or *a special feeling*, while your partner thinks intimacy means *doing things, being together, or having sex.*

It is time to clearly define what intimacy means to you and your partner. You might be surprised to learn you both have very different viewpoints, or you may find them to be very similar, but just different enough to cause some disconnect in your communication. You also might discover that because you have never really thought about it before, you don't know where to begin and can't clearly define intimacy enough to articulate it in your head, let alone in writing to share with your loved one. That's OK too, we've got you covered. Individually, take a few moments now to go through the following exercise to help you clearly define what intimacy means to you.

Intimacy Definition Exercise

This exercise will help you create your own definition of intimacy. For those of you who feel you already have a clear idea of what intimacy means to you, this exercise will refine it and make it crystal clear to you and your partner. For those of you who have never thought about it in this sense, or only have a relatively vague idea, this simple process will give you an opportunity to create clarity for the first time. Regardless of how clear you think you are in your head, challenge yourself to write it down so you can share and discuss it with your partner. The clarity that comes as you complete this step and the final written definition you create will give you the power, energy and confidence to open up to each other and talk about your needs.

In our practice we discovered that when people are challenged to write their own personal definition of intimacy they often surprise themselves as the written end result turns out to be something different than what they originally thought. Rather than the traditional dictionary or popular culture definitions, or what they had read or saw in movies, they explored their own unique needs and created something that felt truly **authentic** to them. In addition, the process of writing created clarity as they honed their definition to only include those things that truly resonated within themselves and was a unique expression and representation, in their own words, of what intimacy meant to them. The result was a definition that created a true foundation on which to build a life-long relationship of the romance and passion they craved.

The exercise for creating your definition of intimacy occurs in three steps. In Step 1 you will review a number of words or phrases that many consider to be important aspects of intimacy. We will then ask you to select only those words and phrases that resonate with you and are most important to you. In Step 2, you will group your selected words into groups of words and phrases that have similar meaning to you. Finally, in Step 3, you will draft sentences using your groups of words to create clear definitions of what intimacy means to you.

Step 1: Select Words and Phrases

To complete this step of the exercise, review the following list of words and phrases. Read through the entire list first and pay attention to how you react (feel) with each one. Do the feelings that each word invokes feel like intimacy to you? If you find there are words missing in this list, add them. Then, go back through the list and mark each one as follows:

A – Absolutely necessary for me and important for intimacy. Truly intimate moments MUST have these...

B – Important for intimacy to me. Intimate moments should have these...

C – Only somewhat important to me. These are nice to have occasionally, but they are not necessary for intimacy nor are they truly important components of intimacy.

- _ Activity (being active)
- _ A certain look (in their eyes)
- _ Adoring them
- _ A feeling of belonging
- _ Attentiveness
- _ Being close (physically)
- _ Being helped (with a task/chore)
- _ Being kissed
- _ Being vulnerable, or feeling they are
- _ Being present (mentally or emotionally)
- _ Being the protector
- _ Caring for them

- Cherishing them
- Complement (complete) one another
- Compliments
- Connection
- Cuddling
- Dancing together
- Dreaming together
- Doing things together
- Doing things for someone else
- Excitement
- Feeling adored
- Feeling appreciated
- Feeling cared for
- Feeling cherished
- Feeling close (emotionally)
- Feeling connected
- Feeling protected
- Feeling respected
- Feeling understood
- Feeling you truly understand someone
- Feeling you are on the same path
- Fun
- Gentleness
- Giving gifts
- Having things done for me
- Hearing or expressing, "I Love You"
- Helping out
- Her scent
- His scent
- Holding hands
- Intensity
- Kissing them
- Knowing they are truly present (attentive)
- Knowing you are in agreement
- Laughter
- Little notes
- Love
- Loyalty
- Passion
- Personal

- Physical contact
- Private
- Quality time
- Receiving gifts
- Respecting them
- Romance
- Sex
- Sexting (racy text messages)
- Sharing a confidence
- Sharing a little secret
- Tenderness
- That little touch as you walk by
- The little things they do
- The little things they say
- The way they communicate with their body (body language and non-verbal communication)
- The look in their eyes
- Togetherness
- Touching and being touched
- Truly knowing someone
- Trusting or being trusted
- Other: _____
- Other: _____

Step 2: Words of Intimacy Grouping...

For each of the values you marked with an "A" in Step 1, take out a pen and piece of paper and organize them into groups of similar or related words and phrases. A word or phrase may appear in more than one group. Simply group them in a way that feels right to you. You should have somewhere between 3 and 10 groupings.

Let's see how Sarah and Bob, our Example Couple #3, completed this exercise. The following tables are Sarah's and Bob's completed lists:

Sarah's Completed and Organized List		
• A feeling of belonging • Connection • Togetherness	• Being close (physically) • Cuddling • Holding hands • Physical contact • That little touch as you walk by • Touching or being touched	• Compliments • Feeling cherished • Hearing or expressing "*I love you*"
• Feeling adored • Feeling cherished	• Fun • Laughter	• Love • Romance

Bob's Completed and Organized List		
• Activity • Doing things together	• Being the protector	• Doing things for someone else • Giving or receiving gifts • Helping out • The little things they do
• Feeling appreciated • Feeling understood • Respecting and feeling respected • Trusting or being trusted	• Fun • Laughter	• Love • Passion • Sex

Step 3: Your Definition of Intimacy...

Once grouped, identify the overarching theme of each group. To do this, look at the words or phrases in the group and select the one that has the most meaning to you. This word or phrase will be the heading or "theme" for the group.

For example, Sarah's first group has *"a feeling of belonging, connection* and *togetherness,"* and she decided that her overarching theme is *"connection"* as that word resonates most with her in this grouping.

Now it's time for you to create one statement or short paragraph that represents each group and provides a definition of what that overarching theme means to you. **Write it down as if you were writing it to share with your partner.** For example, the intimacy definition statement for Sarah's first group of words/themes is:

Connection: *Intimacy is a feeling of togetherness and connection, and a feeling of belonging to one another.*

Complete a sentence for each group. Once complete, you now have a clear definition of what intimacy means to you that is ready to be shared with your partner.

Following are the completed definitions of intimacy for Sarah and Bob based on their example groupings:

Sarah's Definition of Intimacy

- **Connection:** *Intimacy is a feeling of togetherness and connection, and a feeling of belonging to one another.*
- **Touching:** *Intimacy is touching you and being touched by you, and the joy of physical connection.*
- **Hearing It:** *Intimacy is hearing you say the words, "I love you," and other expressions of respect and appreciation.*
- **Feeling Cherished:** *Intimacy is feeling cherished and adored by you.*
- **Fun:** *Intimacy is laughter, fun and good times, created and shared together.*
- **Romance:** *Truly intimate moments are filled with romance and love.*

Bob's Definition of Intimacy

- **Doing Things Together:** *Intimacy is being together and doing things together.*
- **Being the Protector:** *I feel I am being intimate when I am protecting you, holding your hand as we walk, taking your arm on uneven ground, holding you close in large crowds.*
- **Giving of Myself:** *An intimate gesture is helping out, giving things to you, and doing things for you.*
- **Feeling Appreciated:** *I feel closer to you when I feel appreciated, trusted and respected for who I am. Just as I am.*
- **Laughter:** *Intimate moments with you are filled with laughter, and I know you are happy.*
- **Sex:** *The most intimate moments we share are when we are making love.*

Using Your Definitions for Greater Intimacy

These are but only a few examples. Yours may be similar or vastly different. The point is that you take the time to examine and discover what intimacy really means to you, write them down, and then share and discuss that definition with your partner, and vice versa.

Imagine if Bob and Sarah had known this information and shared it years ago. What if instead of blindly doing what he thought was an intimate gesture, Bob provided Sarah with intimacy in the way she understood it, with touch and loving words? What if Sarah understood and appreciated Bob for his intimate gestures (washing her car, going out of his way to bring her a latte, watching out for her and keeping her safe when they walk), knowing that these things supported his definition of intimacy? What if, on occasion, she helped out with those chores or did other things for Bob to connect with him in the way he understands best? They would be feeling happier and more connected in their relationship right now instead of feeling disconnected with moments of resentment.

It all boils down to this... If you desire more intimacy with your partner, it is imperative to understand what that word means to both of you.

It is also important to begin to understand the difference between your definition of (and need for) intimacy and your definitions of (and need for) romance and passion. They ARE different. Intimacy forms the foundation for romance and the desire to be romantic. And it is romantic expressions that create the opportunity for passion to be released. But neither romance nor passion "feel right" when the foundation of intimacy is unstable or is not there at all. So, for now, it is OK if your definition of intimacy includes all three (intimacy, romance, and passion); however, as you begin to use the tools in this book you will naturally discover how romance and passion differ from but are related to intimacy and what each one means to you and your partner. Understanding the differences will create a deeper connection in your relationship. Look for additional tools for expanding your unique definitions of romance and passion and growing your relationship on www.TheCouplesGrowthChallenge.com.

Quite frankly, it all boils down to this… If you crave more intimacy with your partner, it is imperative to understand what that word means to both of you. Once understood, you can open up, accept and experience more daily opportunities (intimate moments) in a way that works best for each of you so you can enhance, maintain, and grow the intimacy in your relationship for a lifetime.

Men and Women are Inherently Different

Besides the obvious physical differences, men and women *are* inherently different. Or, to say it more precisely, men and women are, for the most part, wired differently. As Dr. John Grey brings to light in his books, *Men Are From Mars, Women Are From Venus*, and *Why Mars and Venus Collide*, there is good scientific evidence that shows women have more neural pathways between the brain hemispheres than men. No worries, guys... This doesn't necessarily mean women are smarter than men. This simply means women can have many things going on in their brain at once. Men, on the other hand, tend to be left brain dominant and function better focusing on one thing at a time, a single task. This doesn't make one gender better than the other; it just *is what it is*.

This being said, for most men to be **present** "in the moment," that moment needs to become THE focus. They need to break away from their current activity, whatever it is, and engage with their partner in order to be totally present to facilitate an intimate moment.

For women, in general, in order to be "in the moment," they need to be able to *singularly* focus. Most women have a hundred things on their mind at once. They need to practice letting go of these things **for a moment** so they can focus as completely as possible on that particular moment in order to facilitate an intimate moment with their partner.

For both genders, as best they can, and in their own way, men and women need to focus their attention on their partner in order to create a truly intimate moment with positive results. These intimate moments may last only 8 seconds at a time, but when strung together will create a connection that lasts a lifetime.

It's the same for same sex relationships. Man-to-Man, both need to disconnect from their task and connect with (focus on) their partner to make it an intimate moment. Woman-to-Woman, both need to singularly focus on that moment (hitting the "pause" button on the multiple things on their minds) in order to make a true connection with their partner.

Using Our Differences for Improved Intimacy

For Couple #1, our newly married couple, Ron and Susan, as they go through their life together and begin to settle into a daily routine, the differences between them will likely become more apparent. As an example, Ron is watching a football game on TV one evening when Susan walks through the room and asks him to take care of the dinner dishes for her so she can finish up a report for tomorrow's big meeting. Ron responds without looking up or even thinking about what she said, *"Sure honey. No problem."* Several hours later, his team has a fourth and goal with only 30 seconds remaining in the fourth quarter of a tied game, Susan bursts into the room upset that Ron hadn't taken care of what she asked. Dazed and confused, and still partially focused on the last seconds of the game, Ron tries to recall what Susan asked but can't remember, exactly, what she needed. Both are upset. Ron feels bad because his true intent is to help his wife, but frustrated because he thinks he should be able to watch a football game uninterrupted if he wants to; and Susan feels like Ron ignores her and doesn't care that she needed his help.

Let's see how the Intimate Moment Cycle™ (and what each has learned about the other through this process) can help in this case. First, Susan, knowing that Ron must "break away" from whatever he is currently doing in order to be fully "present," can show love and acceptance by being patient, waiting for him to truly disconnect from the game and connect with her, and not being upset if it takes him a moment or two to make eye contact. Ron, on the other hand, needs to take a few moments to singularly focus on Susan. He might say, "Just a minute honey," and when there is a break in the action, mute the TV and literally turn his body and all of his attention to Susan, ready to truly hear the message, in this case Susan's request. Being present, he can respond and indicate if and when he can take care of what she needs and strike a bargain. The result? A moment of true connection and trust; *an intimate moment*. In addition, Ron can be the helpful guy he wants to be and Susan knows when (or if) Ron will take care of what she needs.

Another example... A few weeks ago, Ron brought home a "just because" gift for Susan. She looked at it hurriedly, set it aside on the kitchen counter and said, "Thanks honey, that was nice! Can you take out the trash? The Johnson's are coming for dinner at 6, and you need to get ready. And before I forget, a statement came in the mail from the bank that looks strange. Can you take a look at it tonight? Oh, and your Mom called and she wants you to call her. She did something to her computer again and needs your help." Ron, dazed and confused, shuffled off to empty the trash and wondered why Susan just blew off the gift he bought her... "She does that every time!" Ron said, under his breath. Susan, on the other hand, was thinking, "That was so nice of Ron; now where did I put the spatula?" Though Susan was truly appreciative, and believed she said so, she didn't realize how devastated Ron was because he felt, from his viewpoint, blown off, unappreciated and completely ignored. He didn't get the reaction he expected, and neither realized they missed an opportunity to create a meaningful, intimate moment together.

Using what we now know, Ron can be more appreciative of the response he did receive, knowing it was heartfelt, and understanding that Susan has much on her mind right now and did not mean to slight his gift. Susan, on the other hand, had she realized this was an opportunity to create an intimate moment, could have become truly present by making Ron and his gift her *singular focus;* letting go, if only for a few seconds, those many other things on her mind. The result would have created an intimate moment, taking mere seconds really, and opened the opportunity to experience warm and positive feelings between them, making a wonderful memory.

What we can all learn from Ron and Susan is that situations that arise like these in our own lives can become intimate moments that strengthen the bond with the one we love if we can appreciate our differences **and** take the 8 seconds needed to connect and complete the Intimate Moment Cycle™.

We Communicate Differently

Each of us has a unique way of processing information and communicating our needs. These inherent differences also impact our intimate communications, both as the communicator and as the receiver. We also tend to communicate in the way we learn best, so understanding our own learning and information processing style and that of our partner's is **vital** to a healthy relationship. Once again, knowledge is power, and understanding our differences will help you communicate most effectively with each other.

Communication is a key factor in the success of any relationship (with your partner, your children, your parents, your boss, co-workers, and friends). The more you can understand your own communication style and that of the person you are communicating with, the better you are able to clearly communicate your thoughts, needs, desires, requests, etc., in a way that works best for both of you.

Though there are a number of theories about communication and learning styles, some simple, some complex, some well accepted, others more controversial; in our practice we like to keep things simple, using concepts that ring true for most people. We use a very simple model, adapted from a model generally attributed to Neil D. Fleming, a secondary and college teacher in New Zealand, showing three basic modes of communication, as follows:

- *Auditory/Verbal:* Learning, processing, and communicating occurs primarily though hearing the spoken word. This includes reading, which for most people is more like hearing the words in their head as they read each word. Auditory learners may often say, *"I hear you,"* when they have received a message effectively regardless of how it was delivered, or may say something like, *"Say that again,"* or *"Tell me again,"* when they need more information. Auditory learners tend to communicate with words, have a fairly extensive vocabulary and, when they get frustrated that you are not receiving the message, might say things like, *"I've told you a million times before!"* In terms of intimate communication, auditory/verbal communicators tend to "say it." They express intimacy by saying, *"I love you,"* and other intimate expressions, and desire to hear it often as well.

- *Visual:* Learning, processing, and communicating occurs primarily through viewing or creating images in their head or on paper, making mind-maps, using demonstrations and body language. Visual learners may often say, *"I see that,"* when they have received a message effectively, regardless of how it was delivered; or may say something like, *"Let me see that again,"* or *"Show me again,"* when they need more information. Visual learners tend to take out a pen and a piece of paper or they go to the white board and draw pictures, sometimes very simple ones, to get a point across. They might point to the drawing again and again and ask, *"Don't you see it?"* when they get frustrated that their message is not being understood. Those who are visual learners need to "see" expressions of intimacy and love in little notes, cards, flowers and gifts, and will tend to express their love in this way as well.

- *Tactical/Kinesthetic:* Learning, processing, and communicating occurs primarily through doing and interacting, touching, and feeling. Kinesthetic learners may often say, *"I feel it,"* or *"I am in tune with you,"* or *"I feel the same,"* when they have received a message effectively, regardless of how it was delivered, or may say something like, *"Give me that again,"* or *"Let me do that again,"* when they need more information. Kinesthetic learners may also withdraw and "close up" when frustrated. They tend to express their intimate feelings by doing things with their partner; going on little outings or trips, or out to dinner and a movie. They also "feel" most loved when their partner expresses their feelings by doing things with and for them as well.

Some people learn and communicate in one very dominant style; and some learn and communicate in more than one style. A few of us can learn and communicate in all styles to a relatively equal ability. And some of us are actually highly deficient in one particular style, so much so, that it might be considered (by some) a learning disability. But for most of us, we figure out how to learn and communicate what we need in our own way and don't give it much more thought. In fact, people naturally assume everyone communicates in the same way they do. So much so that we will tend to think something is wrong with the other person, not in our delivery, when our message is not heard. You've likely heard people say something like (or have said yourself), *"If they don't get me, too bad!"* As you can begin to understand, communication styles can - and do - play a large part in creating meaningful intimate moments. To make a moment intimate, your message needs to be heard and understood in the way that works best for your partner, and vice versa.

Communication for Greater Intimacy

Now that we've discussed differing communication styles, let's look again at our Example Couple #2, Chris and John, to see if we can figure out some of the reasons why they are feeling disconnected.

Remember, Chris thinks it's all about John. Even though John tries, his attempts at creating more intimacy in their relationship always seem to fall short. Why? Chris is an **Auditory** learner while John is **Kinesthetic**. John attempts to be intimate and romantic through *doing* things (both for Chris and for their relationship), planning little outings, and buying gifts for Chris. But what Chris needs is to *hear* how John feels about him. With John communicating in his own communication style, the only thing Chris hears, sees, and understands is John making plans so John can do what John likes to do. Chris would love to *hear* John *tell* him how he feels about their relationship, or to simply say more often, *"I love you."* All this going and doing is fine, but it just ends up missing the mark for Chris when what he needs is John's attentive conversation and verbal affections. John, on the other hand, would love it if Chris took the time to plan some of their outings and did more things for him rather than constantly telling John how he feels about him. **To John, actions speak louder than words. To Chris, words speak louder than actions.**

Can you see the fundamental disconnect in communication styles in this scenario? Each is attempting to communicate in the way they communicate best, rather than in the way their partner best understands the intimate communication. Of equal importance, however, is that neither is appreciating each other's attempts at intimate communication for what it is; an honest attempt at communicating intimacy in the way they know best!

It is important to understand your partner's natural communication style so that you can better recognize their attempts at intimate communications and be appreciative of the effort.

Take a few moments now to discover your communication style as well as your partner's using the quick and simple exercise below.

The Learning Styles Assessment

Individually, take a few minutes to complete the following questionnaire to assess your *general* or basic preferred learning style (visual, auditory, or kinesthetic). Begin by reading the words in the left-hand column. Of the three responses to the right, circle the one that best characterizes you, answering as honestly as possible with the description that applies to you *right now*. Count the number of circled items and write your total at the bottom of each column. Following the questionnaire, we provide additional questions to help you better understand and analyze your results. The answers will offer insight into how you learn and how you likely tend to communicate.

1. When I try to concentrate...	I grow distracted by clutter or movement, and I notice things around me other people don't.	I get distracted by sounds, and I attempt to control the amount and type of noise around me.	I become distracted by commotion, and I tend to retreat inside myself.
2. When I visualize...	I see vivid, detailed pictures in my thoughts.	I think in voices and sounds.	I see images in my thoughts that involve movement.
3. When I talk with others...	I find it difficult to listen for very long.	I enjoy listening, or I get impatient to talk myself.	I gesture and "talk" with my hands.
4. When I contact people...	I prefer to communicate face-to-face.	I prefer speaking by telephone for serious conversations.	I prefer to interact while walking or participating in an activity.
5. When I see someone I have met...	I forget names but remember faces, and I tend to replay where we met for the first time.	I know people's names and I can usually quote what we discussed.	I remember what we did together and I may almost "feel" our time together.
6. When I relax...	I watch TV, see a play, visit an exhibit, or go to a movie.	I listen to the radio, play music, read, or talk with a friend.	I play sports, make crafts, or build something with my hands.

7. When I read...	I like descriptive examples and I may pause to imagine the scene.	I enjoy the narrative most and I can almost "hear" the characters talk.	I prefer action-oriented stories, but I do not often read for pleasure.
8. When I spell...	I envision the word in my mind or imagine what the word looks like when written.	I sound out the word, sometimes aloud, and tend to recall rules about letter order.	I get a feel for the word by writing it out or pretending to type it.
9. When I do something new...	I seek out demos, pictures or diagrams.	I want verbal and written instructions, and to talk it over with someone else.	I jump right in to try it, keep trying, and try different approaches.
10. When I assemble an object...	I look at the picture first and then, maybe, read the directions.	I read the directions, or I talk aloud as I work.	I usually ignore the directions and figure it out as I go along.
11. When I interpret someone's mood...	I examine facial expressions.	I rely on listening to tone of voice.	I focus on body language.
12. When I teach other people...	I draw them a picture or diagram.	I tell them, write it out, or I ask them a series of questions.	I show them how it is done and then ask them to try.
Total	Visual: _____	Auditory/Verbal: _____	Tactile/Kinesthetic: _____

Understanding Your Learning Style Results

Once you have completed the Learning Styles Assessment, answer the following questions to better understand your results:

- Is there a column with clearly a larger number of answers selected? Did you find that you easily answered the questions in that column over the others? If you have a column that has a significantly greater number than the other two, then you likely have a very dominant learning style. That is, you likely need to learn and communicate in that method and may find it difficult to learn in others. This may mean that your partner's communications (including their intimate communications) need to be expressed to you solely in this form for you to really hear, see or feel them fully. This may also mean that you predominantly communicate with others in this method. In terms of intimate communications, the key is whether your partner is, or is not dominant in the same modality!

- Are there two columns with relatively the same number of answers and one column with relatively few? Did you find yourself vacillating between choosing the statements in those two columns? If you have two relatively even columns and one with very few answers, then you likely can learn effectively and receive communications (including intimate communications) in either method, but most likely need to experience both simultaneously to receive the intimate message most effectively.

- Do you have relatively even answers across all columns? If you do and found it difficult to choose between the three columns because all the answers seemed to relate to you, then you might be one of the truly gifted learners who can learn in any modality. Once again, however, the flip side is that you may require all modalities simultaneously to learn and communicate most effectively and to fully receive intimate messages, which can be difficult to achieve in all situations.

- If you find it hard to select one answer in each column because they ALL seem to fit you, take a moment to look back over the exercise. Try to be very clear and pointed in your perceptions as you read through the questions again. Do you find yourself drawn to one answer first and then the others? As an example, one of our female clients took the test and felt that all of the answers seemed to fit her; however, after we used Question #11 as an example for open discussion with her, she realized she was first drawn to the tone of someone's voice and *then* would consider the facial expressions and body language, but because it all happens so quickly for her, she lumped it all together as one impression and found it difficult to choose only one answer. Once she understood this process, even though difficult for her to dissect, she was able to retake the assessment to determine that she has a slightly dominant Auditory learning style. She also discovered that because all the answers seemed to fit that she learns best when combining all three.

Now, ask yourself the following questions to confirm your answers: Do the results align with your past experience? When you think back, what classes in school did you excel in? Did you tend to do well in classes where the teacher presented information in the dominant method suggested by this assessment? What about the classes or teachers you didn't understand? How was information presented to you, all by written hand-out, oral presentation by the instructor, or hands-on interaction? Now think about a work situation. Did you have a boss you "clicked with," or you easily understood and rarely needed additional clarification to perform a task? How did they communicate with you, face-to-face discussion, email directions, or by walking you through a step-by-step process? How about a boss you did not communicate well with? How did they communicate with you? Now think about a family situation or a former partner. Is there a family member you love but can't be around very long because you can't talk to him? Or do you have one child you seem to understand better than another? Is there a former partner where communication was difficult or easy? How did they communicate with you? And finally, how does your partner communicate with you now? How do these situations compare with the results of your assessment? Can you begin to see where misunderstandings can arise as we communicate with one another? We hope you also are beginning to understand how much easier great connections can be made when the communication styles of both parties are more in alignment, or at least understood by both parties.

How does your past experience align with your assessment results? If they align fairly well, then you know your dominant learning style or that you can receive intimate communication fairly well in multiple styles. If on the other hand, you are the rare exception and this assessment did not provide clarity, then the only question is whether you have, in the past, found learning and communicating fairly easy or extremely difficult. If easy, then it is likely you have the ability to use all modalities and you have no true dominant style. This is a good thing as you can easily communicate and receive messages in all styles with most people. On the other hand, if you have found learning and communicating fairly difficult, you may want to consider obtaining an assessment from a specialist to help you better understand your learning and communication style so you can share that information with your partner and others in your life to foster understanding and better communication.

Using Learning Styles to Improve Intimacy

Let's look again at our first example couple, Susan and Ron. Susan is dominant auditory and Ron is visual and kinesthetic. Susan needs to *hear it* and Ron needs to *see it, touch it* or *feel it*. Susan expresses her love for Ron by saying, "*I love you,*" "*I adore you,*" etc. Susan texts it, emails it, and calls periodically to touch base and tell him how she feels. She does not hear it in return as often as she likes from Ron, however. Ron, on the other hand, leaves Susan little notes, buys her gifts, and plans little experiences such as wine tours, and he likes to go on long walks together in the park. Susan finds these outings fun, but they would mean so much more to her if Ron pulled her in close and whispered, "*I love you*" in her ear, like she does to him frequently. Ron certainly likes it when Susan says, "*I love you,*" but she rarely takes the time to get him little gifts or plan special outings. Now THAT would speak volumes to him. It would show him that she really cared about what he likes and that she wants to spend time with him. He knows she loves him; he just doesn't see and feel it as often and as deeply as he would like.

Now that they understand each other's learning style, Ron can now choose to say what he feels more often and Susan can now choose to do more for Ron. As importantly, they can both more easily recognize the attempt at, and desire for, intimacy in what the other says (Susan) or does (Ron). Finally, both Ron and Susan can be more forgiving and laugh off the missed communications, understanding that they are equally responsible for the ultimate success or failure of the message being received. The result is more intimate moments created, more connection and greater appreciation for the love one intends for the other.

There are three things we hope you will learn about learning styles from this information:

- That **everyone communicates and needs to be communicated to differently**. Understanding your own communication needs as well as your partner's will assist you in making your intimate communications more effective and meaningful.

- **You do not need to change who you are** to make your intimate communications more effective. Quite the contrary. You are who you are and being true to yourself is fundamental to a strong and loving relationship. After all, who you are is what attracted your partner to you in the first place! You can, however, make a commitment to learn to communicate in the way your partner needs.

- Perhaps one of the most important things to learn in all this is **appreciation**. By understanding your partner's dominant communication style you can more easily recognize and appreciate their intimate communications for what they are intended to be even though they may not be expressed in the way you need them most.

Now, take some time to share your communication style with your partner. Discuss and understand how *knowing* this information will help strengthen your relationship.

We Are Motivated Differently

Now that you understand your communication style and your partner's, it's also important to understand how you both are motivated. To be motivated is to have a purpose to act; a reason to do something. Regarding a loving relationship, it is the reason for choosing to make intimate gestures, to do something romantic, or to act in a loving way with your partner. One might think that in a truly loving relationship, the motivation to act in a loving way should be a given, a constantly high priority, and to a degree that is true. That is, it should be a given that each partner in the relationship *intends* to act in a loving way. But as the old saying goes, *"the road to hell is paved with good intentions."* What often happens, especially as a relationship matures, is the initial motivation to act in a loving way turns into an assumption that their partner already **knows** how they feel about them and it's not necessary anymore to make the extra effort. In short, and this is important to realize, **we lose the motivation to act because we lose the perception of the need to act.**

So, what do we need to understand about motivation when it comes to creating intimacy? There is considerable research and many theories about motivation. Some of this research centers on the question of *why* we act, and others are focused on *how* we can motivate others to do something we want, particularly in the work environment or in the home as we raise our children. Most of this research ends up providing us with the following conclusions:

- That we, as humans, act to fulfill a need or desire and when needs are satisfied we are no longer compelled or motivated to act. All people have basic needs such as food and shelter, and higher order needs such as love, self esteem, and self actualization. We act to fulfill the basic needs first and once those are met, the higher order needs can be pursued.

- Our need to act comes in two forms. We act to do things we enjoy, or for personal satisfaction, and where there is no promise of a tangible (physical) reward, such as learning for the love of knowledge or saying a kind word to someone who is hurting emotionally. This is called *intrinsic* (or internal) motivation. When we act to receive a tangible reward, however, such as going to work to earn money, doing homework to get good grades, or setting up a romantic date for the sole purpose of getting sex later in the evening, this is called *extrinsic* (external) motivation.

- Long-term and sustaining desire for action occurs only when you are intrinsically motivated and when external factors do not suppress that internal drive. **Motivation, when all is said and done, is really an "inside job."** You must motivate yourself. Someone else cannot do it for you. Yes, you can be "inspired" by others to do great things and external circumstances (such as a fire) can cause you to act, but the desire to act without reward or fear of punishment comes from within.

- In order to reignite your own internal drive for sustaining, long-term and intimate action, it is important to understand how you are *intrinsically* motivated and **that the need for intimate action continues to exist.** This knowledge will help you create situations where the best external conditions exist so your internal drive, your intention for intimacy, can be released most effectively.

- Based on work done by David McClelland,[1] a noted American psychologist, there are three main needs-based intrinsic motivators: a dominant need for *achievement*; a dominant need for *affiliation*; and a dominant need for *power*. McClelland's work, and the research done by those who followed him, indicates that each of us is motivated in all three ways but to

---

[1] David C. McClelland, "Methods of Measuring Human Motivation", in John W. Atkinson, ed., *The Achieving Society* (Princeton, N.J.: D. Van Nostrand, 1961), pp. 41-43.

varying and unique degrees. Further, most of us have one dominant need while some have two rather equally dominant needs, and a rare few are relatively equally motivated in all three. Additionally, McClelland theorized that our unique mix of motivators (or dominant needs) were "hard-wired" in all of us by the age of 17. That is, nature and nurture has created a dominant need that drives our behavior on a consistent and daily basis throughout our lives.

The Keys to Using Motivation to Create Intimacy

The keys, then, for sustaining the motivation to act intimately and romantically, as we all did in the initial stages of our relationship, are as follows:

- **To realize that we still NEED to act**. We need to act to receive the love, attention and affection we need AND to give the love, attention and affection our partner needs. Our needs for intimacy may change, over time (see the next section), but we will always have needs and so will our partner. The bottom line is if you, or your partner, are not getting those needs met, resentment and frustration may set in and, potentially, you or they may begin looking for the love and attention they need somewhere else. That fact alone is pretty darn motivating!

- **To align our good intentions with our natural way of being motivated.** What this means is that as an individual, you must understand your intrinsic motivators so you can tap into them to naturally (easily) create intimacy in your relationship. It is also important to know and understand your partner's motivators and true intention so you both can take action to create a loving situation that does not unintentionally de-motivate one or both of you in your relationship. Later in this section, we provide you with examples of how someone can be de-motivated in a relationship. For now, understand that intention and interpretation (perception) are not the same!

As with communication, therefore, understanding your own as well as your partner's unique motivation style will help you appreciate each other's *intent* to be intimate, and help you create conditions where you are naturally motivated to act in an intimate way.

Types of Intrinsic Motivators

Let's look at the three types of intrinsic motivators in more detail and how they impact the desire to act:

- *Achievement:* People with a high need for achievement have a need to succeed and they seek to excel. They are motivated by setting and achieving objectives and winning and finishing at the top of their class. They have, and set, high standards for themselves. Because they seek to achieve, they also tend to avoid both low-risk and high-risk situations. Achievement-motivated individuals generally avoid low-risk situations because easily attained success is not a genuine achievement, at least in their minds. In relationships, this may mean that acts of intimacy or romance that they interpret as taking little or no effort are typically avoided because they mean little TO THEM. In high-risk situations, those who are achievement-motivated see the outcome as one of chance rather than one's own effort, and consequently avoid taking the risk. Thus, high achievement-motivated individuals would tend to avoid doing something "romantic" if there was not a moderate to high degree of success, with success being a complete and total romantic "high" for themselves AND their partner. High achievement-motivated individuals tend to act when there is a moderate probability of success, ideally 50% or greater. That is, they are NOT risk takers. Achievement-motivated individuals need regular feedback in order to monitor the progress of their achievements, so feedback from their partner on their intimate intentions is necessary and important.

- *Affiliation:* Those with a high need for affiliation need harmonious relationships with other people. They need to feel accepted and feel a sense of involvement and "belonging" within their relationship and their social group. They tend to conform to the norms of their family or work group. High affiliation-motivated individuals prefer relationships that provide significant personal interaction, warm interpersonal relationships, and approval from those for whom they care about. They tend to be supportive family and team members, but may be less effective in taking the lead because of their need to be liked. Some may think those who are affiliation-motivated would make ideal relationship partners because, by definition, they seek close relationships. Seeking close relationships is not the same, however, as ACTING to create closeness. Those who have a dominant need for affiliation will act only when their actions will result in closeness and will refrain from acting if they do not feel that their actions will create what they seek. They rarely act when there is a risk of creating a breakdown of the relationship. In their mind, effort speaks louder than results and they seek approval for their efforts to create intimacy.

- *Power:* A person's need for power can be one of two types - *personal* and *institutional*. Those who need personal power want to direct others, and this need often is perceived as undesirable when it is taken to extreme with the desire to have power OVER others. Persons who need institutional power (also known as social power) want to organize the efforts of others to further the goals of the relationship, family, or organization. In relationships, those with a high need for institutional power tend to act intimately or romantically when they believe their actions will move the relationship in the direction they desire. For example, they may act romantically if they see it will move the relationship closer to having children, which is their view of where the relationship should go. They also avoid actions when they do not believe it will add to their feeling of "control" of the relationship. For example, a person with a high need for institutional power may avoid taking that romantic vacation or buying flowers if it may mean a loss of financial "control" over the relationship. This "control" can be, but is not necessarily, negative or oppressive. Said another way, "control" in the context of those who are motivated by power is NOT necessarily bad or negative.

Discovering Your Natural Motivation

To help you discover how you are naturally motivated, or to confirm what you suspect is your natural motivation style, we provide the following exercise.

To complete this exercise, read the statement in the first column of the table below; then read each of the statements in columns *A* through *C* that potentially completes the sentence. For each possible answer, rate your agreement with the complete statement on a scale of 0 to 10. If you agree completely, rate it a 10. If you don't agree at all, rate it a 0. Rate all three statements, however, the total in all three columns must add up to 10. Read all three possible responses before rating each one.

Example: For the first statement you might place 7 in column *A*, indicating you agree strongly with it; 3 in column *B*, indicating you agree somewhat with it; and 0 in column *C* indicating you do not agree at all with that statement.

Any combination of agreement from 10-0-0 to 4-3-3 is acceptable; however, there will always be one column you are most in agreement with (a minimum value of 4).

Statement	A	B	C
When I work in a group or team...	I feel frustrated with all the talk and just want to get it done myself.	I feel invigorated and really enjoy working together toward a common goal.	I like to be in a leadership role and I tend to take charge in meetings.
I find I do my best work when...	I have clear goals and objectives.	I can work with others and be part of a team.	I am in charge or in a position of authority.
I like to work best...	By myself.	With others.	Managing people or projects.

Statement	A	B	C
When I work by myself...	I feel in control and can best impact the outcome.	I feel less connected to the outcome.	I feel less able to affect the outcome.
When I am called on to be in charge...	I make sure there are clear goals and objectives.	I work to build consensus and buy-in from those I am leading.	I really take charge and lead the group.
The best manager I ever had...	Set clear goals and objectives and provided feedback on progress.	Included me in decisions and made me feel part of the team.	Gave me the project and let me lead.
What gets me up in the morning is...	The opportunity to get things done and tick items off my list.	Working with great people to achieve a common objective.	Being the person in charge and making things happen.
The best job I ever had...	I worked by myself and was rewarded for achieving goals.	I worked with others and enjoyed the camaraderie of my teammates.	I led a project or team that created real value for the company.

Statement	A	B	C
When I set goals for myself...	I almost always reach them. ____	I sometimes reach them, especially when I am accountable to the team. ____	I am the one who sets goals for others. ____
Getting the acceptance and appreciation of others is...	Nice, but really not that important. ____	What I live for. ____	Acceptance? I want respect! ____

SCORING: Add up the values in each column to determine your dominant **intrinsic** motivation style (the one with the largest value), and your secondary **intrinsic** motivation style.

TOTALS: _____ _____ _____

Dominant and Secondary Motivation Style: If the largest or second largest number is:

- Column *A*, you have a dominant (or secondary) need for *Achievement*.

- Column *B*, you have a dominant (or secondary) need for *Affiliation*.

- Column *C*, you have a dominant (or secondary) need for *Power*.

Circle your dominant and secondary motivation styles above.

Note: Any combination of totals may be seen from highly dominant to relatively even. There is no "right" combination. What IS important is what is right for you and whether the results appear to represent how you are truly motivated.

Confirming and Using the Results

Looking at your results from the previous exercises, answer the following questions:

- Think about past activities, jobs, or intimate gestures you really enjoyed where you felt good about what you did. What kind of situation was it? Did it require motivation and action more aligned with Power, Affiliation, or Achievement? Does that align with the dominant motivation styles identified from the completed exercise?

- Now think about previous jobs, activities or things you did in a relationship that you did not enjoy or where you did not feel satisfied by the outcome or what you accomplished. What kind of motivation was required for that work or activity? Does that align with your non-dominant motivation styles?

If you answered *yes* to both questions above, then you can be very confident with your results and you can move on to the next section.

If you did not answer yes to both questions, however, do not worry. Simply answer the following questions:

- Have you been able to effectively motivate yourself in the past when you really needed to get something done? If so, then go through the exercise again and think about those times in the past when you felt motivated. Try to determine if those times of motivation were more aligned with Power, Affiliation or Achievement, or some combination of the three.

- Have you always been able to effectively motivate yourself based on any given situation? If so, this is truly a valuable gift and means you can likely motivate yourself using any or all motivation modalities in your relationship. The bottom line is you don't have a problem with motivation.

- Are you still not certain what your dominant motivation style is? If so, you will need to evaluate yourself in more detail moving forward to come to a conclusion. If this is you, remember - you now have information to help you better understand yourself and your partner; so for you, it is also time to move on to the next step.

Using Motivation to Create More Intimate Moments

Now, consider what these results tell you about how you are naturally motivated and how you can use this knowledge to take intimate and romantic action in your relationship. Use your relationship experience to assist you in answering the following questions:

- What types of ***intimate and romantic activities*** are in alignment with your natural way of being motivated? For example, if you are motivated by Power, you might desire activities that allow you to feel "in charge" of the situation or be in control of managing an experience. A person motivated by Affiliation may desire to take action when they feel they are creating a partnership or contributing to the overall success or depth of the relationship as a whole. For those motivated by Achievement, they might desire activities where they can work independently and their individual efforts directly lead to intimate or romantic results with their loved one.

- What type of ***encouragement or support*** from your partner would best motivate you? For those motivated by Power, having clear relationship objectives that can be managed to, being given the authority over certain aspects of the relationship, and where they are appreciated for taking charge may be best. For those motivated by Affiliation, they may be most naturally motivated to act intimately and romantically with a partner who provides constant positive feedback and praise for what they do for the relationship, regardless of results. Achievers, on the other hand, may best act with a "hands off" partner who appreciates their natural ability to get things done, where there is an agreement on who is assigned a task and what the deadlines are, which allows them, without interference, to get the job done.

- What type of communication or reactions from, or situations with your partner **may actually de-motivate you**? For those motivated by Power, being constantly questioned about "how" something is done or stepping in to help without asking may be de-motivating. For those motivated by Affiliation, they may de-motivated when they feel "obligated" to act or in situations where they consistently do not get recognized for their effort (regardless of results, it is the effort that counts). Achievement motivated individuals may become de-motivated when they are told what should or should not be done and in what order, instead of being left to figure it out themselves.

Let's look at our example Couple #4, José and Carmen. José has a dominant need for power. He is naturally and easily motivated to manage and lead his business, take charge, control processes, and create efficiencies. Carmen is an achiever, a do-er. She makes her list of household chores and errands and begins each day with zest to tick them off one-by-one and get them done. When José returns home, he naturally uses his strengths and expresses his "love" for Carmen by pointing out the many ways she could improve her efficiency by suggesting changes to the order in which she gets things done. But these suggestions, stated with the intent of being helpful and loving, are interpreted by Carmen as demeaning and interfering with her natural motivation to get things done in the way she thinks is best. On the other hand, Carmen routinely schedules date nights, parties and social evenings for her and José and wishes he would be more appreciative of her efforts. She also wouldn't mind it at all if he planned an outing or two now and then. José, however, believes Carmen is "in control" of that part of the relationship and he believes (perhaps mistakenly) that he would have to take over COMPLETE control of this part of the relationship if he began to plan their social calendar. José is in control of the family finances and makes sure Carmen has the money she needs to manage the household, care for the kids and create the beautiful home they have together. He often wonders why Carmen never expresses her appreciation for all the time and effort he puts in to keeping the household budget and taking charge of their finances.

> *What most relationships need is more **doing** what the other **needs** and more **appreciation** of what the other **does**!*

This example shows us that, in terms of expressing intimacy, we tend to act in ways that are in alignment with our own natural way of being motivated and we tend to feel these acts are naturally intimate expressions. The example also shows that we tend to want (or desire) our partner to appreciate actions as we intend them, not realizing that there are other ways for them to be interpreted or perceived. **What most relationships need, however, is more *doing* what the other needs and more appreciation of what the other *does*!** In other words, with an understanding of our own motivation style as well as our partner's, we are better equipped to manage our communications with each other most effectively to garner the results we both need and desire in our relationship.

Creating Your Motivation Profile

Use the information above and the examples for José and Carmen on the following pages to create your "motivation profile" as it affects your relationship. This profile includes the type of intimate and romantic activities and the type of encouragement and support that would allow your natural motivation to be released so you can create intimacy in your relationship. You can use our list of 104 practical ideas for creating intimacy (beginning on Page 95) to assist you as well.

José's Motivation Profile

I have a dominant need for Power and thus am naturally motivated to make intimate and romantic gestures that keep me and the relationship under control. Such actions are paying for vacations, buying flowers, and romantic nights out when I feel the finances are in control and these activities or actions will not throw the budget into chaos.

I tend to act when I perceive the need to move the relationship in a given direction, such as to make Carmen happy when I see her unhappiness affecting the stability of the relationship. I will tend to act more intimately and will feel supported when I am appreciated for taking charge of things (such as paying the bills, getting the cars serviced, planning the kids college costs, etc.) that maintain control, order and stability in the relationship and our life together.

I tend to be de-motivated to act intimately when I am questioned about how things are done or when Carmen steps in to help without my asking.

> ### Carmen's Motivation Profile
>
> I have a dominant need for Achievement and thus am naturally motivated to plan and do intimate and romantic gestures. Such actions are planning outings and trips and "date nights."
>
> I tend to act when I know I can get it done and when there is little risk of it not coming out right. I will tend to act more intimately and feel supported when I am appreciated for getting things done (such as running errands, handling household chores, taking care of the kids, etc.), so that José is free to manage his business.
>
> I tend to be de-motivated to act intimately when I am questioned about what I am doing and in what order I am doing them, and when I feel I am being told what to do.

As We Grow, We Change

It is important to remember, regardless of all the factors we've discussed thus far, that as we grow and mature, so do our needs for intimacy, romance, and passion. We don't mean they simply "diminish" over time as some natural consequence of the aging process. In fact, we believe that a diminished need for intimacy is a myth! Everyone needs intimacy, regardless of our age, gender, or sexual orientation, however, we do believe that our needs for intimacy can, and likely do, *change* over time.

As explored in the book, *Deep Medicine*, William B. Stewart, MD writes about the work of psychologists William R. Miller and Joseph C'deBaca. These gentlemen studied individuals who reported sudden transformative change in their lives. The list below, taken from Dr. Stewart's book, shows the top four sudden transformations that occurred for these men and women as they aged. "Before" relates to what was important to them when they were younger. "After" relates to what is important to them now.

Men's Priority Shifts		Women's Priority Shifts	
Before	After	Before	After
Wealth	Spirituality	Family	Growth
Adventure	Personal peace	Independence	Self-esteem
Achievement	Family	Career	Spirituality
Pleasure	God's will	Fitting in	Happiness

Given these results, it is reasonable to assume that as we transform, grow, and change, our world view and perceptions also transform, grow, and change, and these fundamental shifts in perspective will have an impact on our need and desire for intimacy, romance, and passion. For some, it will be a shift from individualization, independence, and personal needs, to needing to feel happy and more connected in our relationship(s). In this case, our definition of intimacy may change from needing more "cave time," to needing more time together to truly connect. For others, it may be a shift from the need to do outgoing, adventurous activities, to a desire to be involved in more spiritual endeavors separately or together. The types of transformations people can and will make in their lives is endless, thus the potential shift of one's needs for intimacy may change in an equally infinite number of ways. Understanding that change will occur as we age, a solid, healthy relationship, therefore, plans for and accommodates these shifts.

Continuous Change and Continuous Intimacy

Let's look again at our young couple, Ron and Susan, example Couple #1. Today, Ron's need for intimacy centers on being understood for the passion he feels to create a sound financial future for himself and Susan. He feels understood and appreciated when Susan thanks him for managing the family budget, meeting with a financial planner, and investing wisely. But as Ron grows, he may come to realize that wealth accumulation without spiritual alignment no longer makes sense to him. So, now his needs shift from a focus on wealth accumulation to a need for something more outside himself. He will still need to feel loved and understood during this shift, even, perhaps, before he fully understands it himself. Thus, consistent, ongoing reflection, discussion and communication of one's need for intimacy is a foundational concept in a strong and lasting relationship.

Keep in mind, all this change can be particularly tough, especially for guys. Men tend to want to solve the problem, fix it once, get past it, and get on to the next thing. They also look at this "intimacy thing" and think... "OK, I can get through this. I

> **Guys** ~ *If you take away one thing from this book, take this... Intimacy is the foundation of your relationship and it's always a work in progress! It's never "one and done!"*

will figure it out, make a game plan, work it through, and I won't have to worry about it again. Done!" That's usually how guys think, right? Identify the problem, fix it, and move on. But when it comes to intimacy, it's NEVER *one and done!*

Guys, we just need to get that into our heads! The key to a long-term relationship is *continual* communication, adaptation and change regarding your own and your partner's need for intimacy.

Lest you think we have forgotten you, we have a message for the gals as well. **Clarity**! In order to get the intimacy you need and desire TODAY, you need to clearly define what intimacy means to you, clearly communicate that to your partner, and show honest appreciation for it when you get it. Yes, your needs will likely change over time as well, and it is important to communicate these changing needs to your partner. Dropping hints or communicating vague ideas will not cut it. Choose what intimacy means to you and clearly communicate that to your partner, remembering the intent of both is to be intimate.

The good news is, we have provided the tools here to help you narrow down your choices to what is truly important to you; and we have provided ways for you to communicate those needs in a way your partner can understand. Feel free to revisit the previous sections and exercises of the book at any time to touch base, reconnect, refresh, and update your definition of intimacy at any time in your life as you grow and change during the course of your journey together.

From Theory to Practice

"Practice means to perform, over and over again in the face of all obstacles, some act of vision, of faith, of desire. Practice is a means of inviting the perfection desired."
- Martha Graham

In the following sections, we provide 104 tried-and-true examples and a few new ideas for creating your own intimate moments. Since many of these examples are not new, the beauty here is that you likely already KNOW them and that they can be repeated often! You not only know them, you're likely **doing** many of them already, but are simply missing one or two of the steps in making it a truly intimate moment by completing the connection using the Intimate Moment Cycle™!

Now that you understand the importance of completing the Intimate Moment Cycle™, you can see things in a little different light. We've just taken what you already know, added some better understanding of yourself and your partner, and shifted your old thought process a mere fraction of a centimeter. It's like a puzzle piece that sat slightly askew before but now fits perfectly in place to complete the puzzle. You now know the secret to getting more of what you want in your relationship!

We also organized the list of examples and suggestions into various themes to remind you that there are many ways to be intimate every day and to show you how easy it can be. You only need to remember to *stop* when you recognize an opportunity and allow yourself to go through the Intimate Moment Cycle™. Remember, it takes two to tango here... One to create the intimate moment, and the other to recognize and be present in it. If you both, as a couple, make the commitment together to being "givers and receivers," you will find your days filled with intimacy which will create the opportunity for romance and ignite the passion you crave.

Also, as you review and discuss these 104 suggestions in the sections below, you will quickly see that many of the ideas being described take longer than 8 seconds. For example, an 8-second walk

> *The simple point is this... Regardless of what the intimate gesture or activity is, to truly make it an intimate moment, you must complete the Intimate Moment Cycle™.*

is not much of a walk! The "8 seconds" we speak of refers to the time it takes to connect and complete the Intimate Moment Cycle™. The simple point is this... Regardless of what the intimate gesture or activity is, to truly make it an intimate moment, you must go through and complete the Intimate Moment Cycle™. It is all about recognizing the moment, being present, truly listening to the love being given, responding to it, and showing appreciation. That cycle, regardless of the intimate activity, can occur in as little as 8 seconds.

To help you to remember the process and put it into practice, we have devised a little pneumonic: B-CLR (or "be-clear"). It means that whenever you **recognize** an intimate moment (which is the first step in the cycle), to complete the cycle you simply need to:

- **B**e present in the moment by disconnecting from what you are doing.
- **C**onnect with your partner using eye contact, touch, etc. and let them know you are engaged.
- **L**isten intently (yes, with both ears) to the message, the deeper message beyond the obvious.
- **R**espond with appreciation and thanks.

Let's look at this again. To remember the steps of the Intimate Moment Cycle™, you first **Recognize** it for what it is then you B-CLR (be-clear); **B**e present, **C**onnect, **L**isten and **R**espond! Kind of silly, we know, but this is about making intimate moments more fun and a little silliness never hurts.

Finally, use the following ideas as a way to discuss and talk more about what intimacy means to you. Discuss the ones that feel intimate to you as well as the ones that don't, and ask each other why. Don't worry if some of them don't float your boat. That's OK. As they say in baseball, *"It only takes one!"* The very act of reviewing the list together is, in itself, an intimate moment (see #33) and who knows where it might lead. The point is that talking through them is a great way to learn about - and continually refresh - your understanding of your needs for intimacy and those of your partner.

It is our hope that this little book, and this simple little process, will help you savor more - and miss fewer - opportunities to create your own intimate moments. We wish you nothing but intimacy filled days and more than your share of romance and passion filled nights! Enjoy the following ideas and feel free to create some new ideas of your own.

Touch

> *"At the touch of love everyone becomes a poet."*
> Plato

Discover the wonderful power of touch, the true connection...

1. **Sit here baby!** Sit close together while watching TV. No words are needed, just be near and be close. Feel the body heat. During a commercial, make eye contact and whisper, "This feels nice," or simply snuggle in closer. It's even OK to make-out during the commercials! Enough said.

2. **Hold my hand.** You can do this anytime, anywhere. Grab your partner's hand and give a little squeeze. And give a squeeze in return! Nothing says more about the intimacy in your relationship than holding hands when you are out and about.

3. **Reach out and touch me.** Reach out and touch your partner as you walk by. It is that simple. Anytime you walk by, just reach out and gently slide your hand over a shoulder, an arm, their backside. Giver's choice! You can even do this during meals whether at home or out with friends, at breakfast or dinner, just reach out and touch a hand, an arm, or find their leg under the table – just make sure it's your partner's! Adding a

moment of connection with your eyes over the table and a little knowing smile adds the icing to this cake.

4. **The first and last hug of the day.** What a great way to start and end every day! Give each other a hug, before or after you get out of bed in the morning – or both! Then grab them at bedtime and snuggle in close. Who knows where it might lead.

5. **Slide on over here!** Sit next to each other - on the same side of the table - when going out for a meal. Share an appetizer while telling funny stories and laugh out loud. Talk about an intimate moment shared in the past and whisper the details to each other. Everyone around will surely be jealous!

6. **Drive by touch.** In the car, just reach over and rest your hand on their leg. Nothing more needed, maybe a little squeeze of the hand and an acknowledging glance. Anything more might cause an accident!

7. **A cranium sensation.** Gentle scratching or a scalp massage feels wonderful after a long day. Of course, be mindful. This may not be their favorite thing in the world or they may not want you to mess up the "do." But for many, this simple act evokes relaxation and the opportunity to experience a little slice of heaven on earth.

8. **Don't forget the feet!** Pay attention to the tootsies! Easy to do while talking about the day or watching an old movie together. With or without lotion, this is another opportunity to bring pleasure and relaxation into your partner's day. We don't recommend tickling, but you could *threaten* to tickle to get something desired, like an "I love you," or a kiss in thankful appreciation.

9. **Give 'em a rub.** Not only has the benefits of massage been touted to promote good health and reduce stress, it helps bring couples closer together as well. Whether a gentle shoulder or back massage or a naked hot oil full body rub down, if it feels good – do it!

10. **Scratch the back.** There's nothing like getting your back scratched and returning the favor! It just feels oh so good and much more effective than looking like a bear against a tree! End this moment with a big thank you and don't forget the bear hug!

11. **The ultimate connection.** Sit facing one another, hold hands and stare into one another's eyes. See how long you can do it without laughing... or see where it may lead!

Taste

> *"What I do and what I dream include thee,
> as the wine must taste of its own grapes."*
> Elizabeth Barrett Browning

The taste of things, and the taste of each other...

12. **Meals for two (or more).** There is nothing like sharing a meal together, being present in those moments, eating good food, and enjoying each other's company. Sharing breakfast begins the day with a moment of connection and communication that not only sets the tone but sustains the bond throughout the day. Sharing dinner, perhaps illuminated with a candle and a focus on connection, sets the stage for a nice evening – whether you spend the rest of the evening together or apart. Even if you share your table with half-asleep toddlers, rowdy teenagers, or a persistent "little Hoover on four legs," it is possible to lock eyeballs on each other for a few seconds and exchange an intimate moment, a raised eyebrow and a smile that only you two can share. Develop your own signal, like a wink, or pulling your ear lobe while looking at your partner, to say, "I love you," while passing the salad.

13. **The lunch date.** You both work hard. Take a midday break once in a while and meet for lunch, if that's possible. It doesn't have to be fancy or break

the bank. It's simply about creating a few moments of togetherness during a busy day. Or pack a lunch and have an impromptu picnic in the park. Not possible to meet during lunch? Agree to eat lunch "together" anyway. Commandeer a conference room at work and eat at the same time while talking with each other on the phone. Cell phones make this possible anytime, anywhere. Whether together in the park or "together" on the phone, remember to take a few seconds in the beginning or at the end to connect and appreciate this time together.

14. **Tea for two.** The Japanese tea ceremony is all about focusing on the moment. And the English have their high-tea tradition that makes people pause during their day and come together. We think there's something to be said about taking a moment to stop whatever you are doing and simply connect for a cup-a-something, even just a few sips, and focus on each other.

15. **Happy hour.** Explore the happy hour specials in your area with your partner. You can find some pretty good deals out there! As with coffee or tea, the idea is to use that time as an opportunity to step back, connect, and focus on each other before heading home.

16. **Happy hour at home.** No good happy hours in your neighborhood? No problem! Make one at home. Break out the vino and cheese plate, or beer and chicken wings! Libations and appetizers will be

served during the 5 o'clock hour every Wednesday, to share together while talking about the day. You can even make this a family affair complete with apple juice and fish-shaped crackers. It is sure to be a hit with the kids and something everyone will remember for a very long time.

17. **Breakfast in bed for two.** Though this one takes a bit more planning, it will likely be highly appreciated by that special someone who does most of the cooking for everyone else.

18. **Cook together.** Cook a favorite meal together, doesn't matter what. Licking fingers is not optional! And dancing together in the kitchen while things are simmering is an added treat.

19. **Share a dessert.** Sharing a single desert, can range from simply delicious to downright sensual. Whether one spoon or two, the pleasures of your favorite desert, shared, while focusing on each other's enjoyment, can truly make an intimate moment.

20. **Feed me.** We know, this is so "over the top" corny, but feeding each other with your fingers really can make for a very intimate and sensual moment, and it doesn't have to be grapes! Any food can be used. Even a juicy, two-handed, bacon double cheeseburger has been known to have almost orgasmic results! The idea is to focus on the pleasure of your partner and share the experience.

21. **Taste that special little spot.** Most of us have a favorite little spot we like on our partner (and we are not talking about *THOSE* spots!). It could be the nape of the neck, the crook of an arm, an earlobe, or the back of the knee. Go ahead - nibble that spot and tell them it's your favorite! Lean in from behind and mount a surprise attack - nosh on their neck, or take their hand and gently bite a finger and simply say, *"Yummy."* No slurping please, a little nibble goes a long way!

Smell

> *"A good fragrance is really a powerful cocktail of memories and emotion."*
> Jeffrey Stepakoff, *The Orchard: A Novel*

Scents can rekindle memories and build powerful connections that will be remembered forever...

22. **Illuminate me.** Whether at dinner, in the bedroom, or just because, light a candle with your favorite scent. There's just something about the softness of candle light and the presence of fire that sets the mood for connection. The scent will seal the memory.

23. **Chanel or Dior, Drakar or Old Spice?** It doesn't matter. If your partner has a favorite scent you wear, wear it gently. A little dab will do ya! Let them know how much you appreciate the way they smell.

24. **"Scent" a note.** Spray a touch of your perfume or cologne on a hand written note for them to find later. You might say something like, "I left a little of me here with you - just to keep me on your mind." Guaranteed to stir a memory, garner a smile, a sniff, a happy sigh, and a big *thank you!* Who knows, you may even find a 'fragrant' little note tucked away for you to find tomorrow.

25. **Sweet sweat.** *IF* you enjoy working out together and the pheromones are agreeable, by all means – do so! There is something very powerful about the true scent of your partner, a bit musty – manly or feminine – almost wild... However, when enough is enough – it eventually turns to stink! That's when you...

26. **Hit the showers... together.** Warm water + soap suds = good times! Grab your favorite smelling body wash and lather each other up! Draw a heart in the steam on the shower door and don't forget your initials! We'll let you figure out the rest with this one...

27. **Cook together.** This one bears repeating as it combines smell and taste! Cook a favorite meal together, breathe in the aromas, talk, connect, laugh, and then enjoy your meal made with love. And remember, nibbling on favorite spots while cooking is not optional! It's a good way to keep the kids out of the kitchen until dinner time... they will surely smile as they exit quickly, stage left. Just be careful around the burners!

A Few Little Words

"Words have power. They work. That's why poetry can affect people. That's why music and lyrics and songs affect people, and that's why chants and prayers and affirmations and all those various things affect the frame of mind."
Sammy Hagar

It is the little things you say that mean so very, very much. When it comes to words, a little can say a lot…

28. **"I love you."** This is a no-brainer, but sadly, one that is often missed or over used without the most important part – connection! Saying, "I love you," while looking into each other's eyes at random moments means so much more because it says you were not only thinking about them but thinking about how you *feel* about them. "I love you" is not only for times of romance, or after sex, and not simply the last thing said as you run out the door. **Stop**, connect (look into each other's eyes), and say it with meaning and a soft touch of your hand to their face. Guaranteed to evoke a spark or two!

29. **"Good morning… Good night…"** Followed by a pet name – or something silly, will wake up their brain almost as good as coffee! (Well… almost!) Say, "Good morning, buttercup!" What? Buttercup? Really? Let your imagination run with this one. And then remember to end the day expressing your love for your partner, "Good night, my love," … or

"Good night, my little rose petal," creates a connection that lasts through your dreams over night. The sillier the better, or not. A simple "Good night, my love," goes a long way.

30. **Always – good-bye and hello.** Whether your good bye's are simple such as, "I love you, see you tonight;" or more elaborate, worthy of Shakespeare, "My love, I shall miss you with every ounce of my being and with each passing moment, until we meet again..." Heck, just quote Shakespeare, *"Parting is such sweet sorrow..."* Make them even more intimate and meaningful by looking into each other's eyes, feeling that connection first, before running out the door. Take the 8 seconds to truly connect, and THEN go about your day. And remember, to reconnect when you see each other again. "Hi, honey, I really missed you today," followed by the 8 second kiss! Go ahead, give that one a try, and make it count!

31. **"I adore you because..."** Look them in the eye and tell them you adore them, but most important, tell them WHY. Is it their heart, their soul, the look in their eyes when they dance or play baseball, the good works they do, or how they interact with the kids? Or is it because they haven't forgotten the little kid in themselves, or the way they respect their parents? It doesn't matter what it is, and it could be many things, just let them know.

32. **Share a good story.** Find an interesting article in the newspaper or your favorite magazine that has meaning to you. Share it with your partner by reading it out loud. It needn't be a novel and it's best to keep it short. Then, tell your partner why this has meaning to you, and ask them what they think.

33. **Read an intimate book together.** If you're reading a novel and come across something of interest, perhaps something suggestive or a bit racy *(wink-wink)*, take a moment and read it out loud to your partner. Or take turns reading from a juicy romance novel or sensual story to spice things up in your relationship. You can also visit our website, www.TheCouplesGrowthChallenge.com, for more information about our Passionate Pursuits™, which we introduce to you at the end of this book, guaranteed to add some fun and excitement, and perhaps a little something out of the ordinary.

34. **Positive adjectives that fit.** Your partner has many great attributes. What are they? Create a list of adjectives and use one of them randomly. Simply say, "You are so loving! Just thought you should know." This is sure to bring a smile of wonder to your partner's face along with a simple, "Thank you." They will love you for noticing!

35. **I believe in you.** When you express your trust in their abilities and that you respect them for who they are, you are not only helping them build confidence in themselves, but confidence in the underlying

foundation of your relationship. Saying, "I believe in you," is very powerful.

36. **Remembering a special occasion.** Yes, we are talking about the biggies; birthdays, anniversaries, etc. But it also might mean remembering the hike you took when you realized you were in love with each other. Or it might be a special milestone or achievement such as the birth of your first child, or graduating with your Masters. Whatever it is, acknowledge it in a way your partner understands. If this one is difficult for you because you tend to forget these things, enter the dates in the calendar and set a reminder on your cell phone (or some other calendar system). You'll be the hero going forward.

37. **Sharing a memory in words.** These moments can begin with, "Do you remember when...?" They can also start with, "I remember when..." Either way, you are sharing a part of you with your partner that either has meaning to you individually, or to you as a couple, and it will bring you back to the foundation of your relationship – your memories together.

38. **The laughs on us.** It can be a very intimate moment when the two of you share a private joke and giggle uncontrollably while everyone around you thinks you both must be crazy! When you discover these private jokes, keep them to yourself and "trigger the giggles" whenever you can.

39. **Little love notes.** Briefly mentioned above (in "Scent a Note"), periodically put a love note in a pocket, on a pillow, or stick a note to the driver's seat in the car, the bathroom mirror, or in the book they are reading. Wherever you know they will eventually find the note, leave one. It can be as simple as, "I love you," to as racy as, "I want to bite your _____!" (You fill in the blank!) Just make sure they're the one to find it and not their boss or your kids…

The Kiss

> *"When you kiss me, without uttering a single word,
> you speak to my soul"*
> Unknown

The sweet, sensuality of a kiss, in oh so many flavors... Kissing is, by definition, intimate, but there are lots of ways to spice it up, change it up, and keep it fresh. Just remember to connect with your eyes when you come up for air..

40. **The little smooch.** Even the quickest, lightest kiss can have meaning if you stop, connect with the eyes, acknowledge, and deeply appreciate it!
41. **The 30-second kiss.** Go ahead! Give them a long, deep one. Lavish the moment, savor the softness of their lips, the taste of their mouth, the feel of their body so close to yours. It's OK to lose yourself in a kiss. Really it is!
42. **The passionate kiss.** Hold on to your hat! This is a good, firm kiss that leaves no doubt about how you feel. Where it leads... well... that's totally up to you.
43. **The hello kiss.** Don't just verbally say hello, say "Hello, handsome/gorgeous, I missed you today and I think you are wonderful," with your lips. Say it all in your kiss.
44. **The good-bye kiss.** And don't just verbally say good-bye. Give them a good-bye kiss that they'll think about for the rest of the day!

45. **The surprise kiss.** Give them a kiss when they least expect it. Go ahead, just lean in and plant one on 'em! It's not like you have to have a reason! Right?

46. **Kiss that special little spot.** This one bears repeating as well, as mentioned in "Taste." Most of us have a favorite little spot on our partner (and, again, we are not talking about *THOSE* spots). Whether the nape of a neck, the crook of an arm, behind the ear, or the curve of a shoulder. Go ahead, lean over and kiss that spot and tell them why you like it!

From a Distance

> *"Absence is to love as wind is to fire;*
> *it extinguishes the small and kindles the great."*
> Roger de Bussy-Rabutin

When you are apart, whether across town for work or across the country, you can make intimacy happen, anytime, anywhere...

47. **The phone call.** This old standby never fails. Give them a call, even if you have to leave a message just to say hello, to connect, or to say anything you want. The point is to make that connection! It's OK to discuss the grocery list, or confirm the plan to pick up the kids after school, just remember to begin and end the call on an intimate note... "Hi, honey, I was just thinking about you and had to hear your voice... chit chat... chit chat... chit chat... OK, hon, I can't wait to see you tonight. I love you."

48. **The E-mail.** Like the phone call, the e-mail provides you the opportunity to connect and say anything you want. But remember to keep it "PG" if you are using work email addresses. Big Brother IS watching!

49. **The greeting card.** When one of you is away for a while, sending or receiving a greeting card is always a treat. There are so many to choose from! Even if no one goes anywhere, finding a "just because" card in the mail with your name on it, sent by your

partner who was thinking of you when they sent it, is pretty darn special.

50. **The E-card.** Need more of an instant delivery card? Try e-cards. There are free and pay e-card services on line and there are plenty that say just exactly what you want to say in that moment.

51. **Send a picture of yourself.** Share a moment with your partner, even when you are not together. Snap a picture with your smart phone and hit *Send*. You could be at an event, wishing they were there. Or you could send a "suggestive" photo, if you dare, or a picture of a spot on you and make them guess where it is.

52. **The text message.** Anything fun and suggestive you might want to say in person can be said in a text or a private tweet. You could write an entire book about the art of texting (or sexting) and tweeting your partner. Let your imagination run wild, and prime the pump during the day with affirming and suggestive text messages such as, "I am so in love with you..." Or, "So desire you right now... What time will you be home?" Just make sure you're sending your text to your partner and not your mother or your boss. Yikes!

Something For Him

> *"You give but little when you give of your possessions.
> It is when you give of yourself that you truly give."*
> Kahlil Gabran

Something just for him... Remember, every man is different. This is about what your man needs and some of these ideas may not fit him. It's OK to revise or create your own to meet your partner's needs...

53. **When he's watching the game on TV**, kiss the top of his head, tell him you love him and that you hope he enjoys the game. Better yet, sit down next to him and watch it with him. (Careful with this one. If you sit down, don't talk about anything else but the game. He likely won't hear you and may even get frustrated with the interruption.) Sit there and read a book or something if you're not interested in the game and enjoy the moments when he reaches out to touch you, or wants to share a great play with you... "Did you SEE that? Watch the replay!" If you absolutely can't stand it, give him a kiss during a commercial break, tell him you love him and enjoy the game. Then go share some girl time with a friend. He will still appreciate knowing that you're OK with him watching the game. You're not giving him permission, that's his choice, but it's an intimate gesture on your part to let him know you're OK with it and happy he's happy.

54. **Get him a drink.** When he is sitting and enjoying the game, offer to get him a drink. Yes, we know how stereotypical, and perhaps a bit Neanderthal this may sound to you, but if it is done willingly as a gesture of giving, without being asked, he will find this a truly intimate moment and will be very appreciative.

55. **Be OK with cave time.** As Dr. John Grey wrote in *Men are From Mars, Women are From Venus*, "Men need cave time," which means time alone, often in their "man cave," that special place in the house that is uniquely theirs. (Some women need alone time as well!) The point is that men often need to tune out for a few minutes before they can be truly present with you later. Your partner will find it a special intimate moment when you acknowledge and encourage this when he needs it.

Something For Her

> *"The value of a man resides in what he gives and not in what he is capable of receiving."*
> Albert Einstein

Something just for her... Again, every woman is different. This is about what your lady needs and some of these ideas may not fit. It's OK to revise or create your own to meet your partner's needs...

56. **Sneak up behind her**, put your hands over her eyes, whisper, "Guess who loves you?" in her ear and kiss her neck.
57. **Run her a bubble bath.** Run her a nice hot bath, light some candles, and turn on some relaxing music. Let her know it is OK to take some time for herself to relax and escape in the bubbles for a little while.
58. **Open the door for her.** When you are out and about, open the car door for her. Open the door to the restaurant, etc. She will appreciate the thought and the gesture.
59. **Go for a walk with her.** Hold hands and walk. You don't even have to talk unless it's warranted. Just take care to make sure she is on the safe side, away from on-coming cars. She will appreciate that you're looking out for her safety.

Around the House

> *"Home is the most popular, and will be, the most enduring of all earthly establishments."*
> Channing Pollock

Intimacy can occur in any room in the house…

60. **Something to drink.** When working on something at home (mowing the lawn, paying the bills, ironing shirts, cleaning the house, etc.), bring your partner a beverage. Sure to be appreciated! The intimate moment is created when they stop, recognize, respond, and appreciate with a touch, a hug, a kind word in return, or a kiss.
61. **The sticky note.** This one bears repeating as well, write a special love note on a sticky note and leave it somewhere you KNOW they will find it (inside the medicine cabinet door, inside their day planner, on the steering wheel, in a book they are reading, etc.).
62. **Help them with a chore.** Is there a chore your partner normally does? Vacuuming, mowing the lawn, doing the dishes or cooking? Volunteer to help them with it and share the effort, or sincerely appreciate it by letting them know what a great job they did when they're done!

63. **Volunteering to do a chore.** Go one step further and volunteer to do it for them. This is especially important when one partner is feeling overloaded and overwhelmed. Just take one thing off their plate and they will feel so much better.

In The Bedroom

"Just leave a trail for me to follow you into the bedroom."
Dierks Bentley

Well, of course, but it is more than what you think…

64. **Warm the sheets.** Instead of just getting into your side of the bed, get in on their side and warm it up for them. Nothing like getting into a toasty warm bed in the winter. They WILL thank you for it. We wouldn't recommend this in the summer time, however.
65. **The pillow fight.** If you're feeling a bit impish, start a good natured pillow fight or a wrestling match. Both can be very intimate and FUN while being a good lead into even more intimate close quarter encounters…
66. **Pillow talk.** Whether just before going to sleep or as you wake in the morning, just spending a few moments talking nose to nose and connecting in bed can be extremely intimate.
67. **The quickie.** Yep, that is exactly what we mean. It can be fun and exciting, especially if you have guests arriving in a few minutes, or while the kids are watching TV! Plenty of intimate moments to be had following *the act* with a wink of an eye and a knowing smile shared with your partner over the heads of your guests or your kids.

68. **Just cuddling.** Spooning, wrapping up together and getting as close as possible. No words needed. Just relax and enjoy.
69. **Help them undress.** Even if you just unbutton his shirt or help her unzip her dress, these can become very special intimate moments with a kiss here and there, or a soft touch.

Out and About

> *"Some people come into our lives and quickly go.
> Some stay for awhile and leave footprints on our hearts.
> And we are never, ever the same."*
> Unknown

Create intimacy when you are out and about on the town or just around the corner from home…

70. **Take a walk.** Whether around the neighborhood, in a park, or along the water, just head out for a stroll. The fresh air and the opportunities for improved communication and connection can be as long as the walk itself. No worries here. It's not about "making" the entire walk an intimate moment. It's simply about taking 8 seconds to create "an" intimate moment during your journey. Remember, even if you need to reject the invitation to go, this too can become an intimate moment depending on how you respond. Remember, recognize the moment then "be clear;" **B**e present, **C**onnect, **L**isten and **R**espond! After recognizing the moment and turning to look at your partner, you may want to respond like this, *"Thank you for asking, honey. I would really love to go, but need to finish what I'm working on first. I'll be done in 30 minutes! Let's go then?"* You can see this is a much better response than, "No, I'm busy," without even a glance. That

kind of response is viewed by your partner as outright rejection. Ouch!

71. **Take a drive.** Hop in the car and head somewhere, anywhere, or nowhere in particular, it really doesn't matter. You can run an errand together or go for a drive along a nice stretch of road to discover a new hole-in-the-wall restaurant. Again, no worries. It's near impossible to make every second an intimate moment, but if you can create even one intimate moment during this adventure together, you will make a positive memory and strengthen your foundation of intimacy.

72. **Watch a sunset.** Got a beach, great! No beach, no view, no problem! There is likely a place nearby with a view of the sunset somewhere, and if not, just sit outside and enjoy the change from light to dusk and the way the sun paints the sky as it fades. Just sitting close together makes it an intimate moment, especially when you lean into each other for warmth as the night chill fills the air. Or talk about a memorable sunset you experienced together before. Give it a try!

73. **Watch a sunrise.** Like sunsets, a sunrise and the experience of watching and hearing the world wake up around you as you sip a hot cup-a-something, can be very intimate indeed. Don't forget to touch!

74. **Watch the stars, clouds or weather.** Whether a stormy day or beautiful clear night, there is always something to watch outside and to wonder about the power and greatness of the universe. Talk about what you see, or feel, or simply breath it all in together in awe.
75. **Buy tickets for an event and call your partner with the news!** Get tickets for the comedy club, a show, or sporting event. The intimate moment is in sharing the news AND the experience of the event itself!
76. **Surprise reservations.** Along the same line, surprise your partner with reservations for dinner tonight. No cooking, no dishes, just time together to connect, to touch, to talk to laugh...
77. **Surprise delivery.** Whether it is flowers, a basket of fruit, or a pizza so they don't have to cook after a long day at work, surprise them with a delivery wrapped up in love, and a note or spoken, "I'm thinking of you..."
78. **Dressing up.** Going out? Take some time to dress the part and make it feel special. Not only can being out and about and all dressed up create an intimate moment, but the act of dressing (and undressing later) can create intimate moments as well. Use your imagination here... Remember when you were first dating – how you agonized over what to wear to evoke a desired positive response? Remember when – and do it again! And if you're on the receiving end, respond accordingly. A "WOW" response, or

sincerely and utterly speechless, will get you a very long way!

79. **Volunteer together.** When you focus on meeting the needs of others as a couple, such as volunteering at your local food bank, adopting a family at Christmas, getting involved in Rotary together, or building a school in Belize, etc., you can create a very powerful memory that can deepen and strengthen your relationship beyond what you can imagine. You will be proud of what you accomplished together and share many intimate moments talking about the experience. Give it a try!

Just Between the Two of Us!

"Other than intimacy with a loved one is there any better feeling than knowing that you're so close or better still, right next to the one you truly love."
Danny Santagato

Those little things that are just "our little secret..."

80. **Finding a secret word for sex that only the two of you share.** Imagine having an engaging conversation about hot and spicy "Bar-b-que" around a group of friends when you are really talking about what you will do later when you get home! Fun, and very secretly intimate!

81. **Create a "trigger" word.** Come up with your own "prompt" to trigger an intimate moment to connect with each other. (Remember, we mentioned the expression from the movie, *Avatar*, earlier in the book... "I see you.") Yours could be something from a favorite book, an old movie, or even something silly. What matters is that whatever "it" is, it triggers the response you desire – connection. Enjoy!

82. **Express appreciation.** Saying thank you for something your partner has done can be made into an intimate moment by simply taking a moment to complete the cycle... Lock eyeballs, connect, respond! Damn, that's easy! To make an even greater intimate moment, let them know how much

you appreciate them, "just because" when they least expect it.

83. **The look.** Whether lustful, playful, or a look of love or wonder, this is "the look" understood by both, when shared, and recreates the feelings and connection behind its meaning.

84. **The compliment.** Whether it is something they have done, or how they look in that moment, or the way they dressed today, a sincere compliment is always a big hit and a nice little "deposit" in the love bank!

85. **Listening, really.** Whatever you are doing, stop, disconnect from it, and really, truly and completely focus on what your partner is saying. You both *know* when the connection is made. ZING! That's it! Enjoy!

86. **Share their hobby.** Does your partner have a hobby? Share it with them now and again. Even if you only talk about it with them. Showing interest in what they are interested in (regardless of how you feel about it) speaks volumes about how much you care for them.

87. **Remember the moment you fell in love and mention it.** When you are day dreaming about that moment, just mention that you are. Or talk about the first time you met and the little things you remember about that day. The memory will definitely bring a smile and some warm feelings for both of you!

88. **Express one of the many reasons why you love them.** "How do I love thee, let me count the ways..." Paraphrasing Elizabeth Barrett Browning's poem, there are many reasons why you love your partner. Make a list and share one every now and then.

With Others

"As you grow older, you will discover that you have two hands, one for helping yourself, the other for helping others."
Audrey Hepburn

Intimate moments can be made and shared even in a crowded room full of people you know, or don't, and even when your house is *chaos on wheels* with children...

89. **Play with your kids, together.** If you have kids, play with them together. Smile and laugh with your baby or play board games with your older kids. The connection with you as a family can be a wonderfully intimate moment between the two of you as you meet each other's eyes and smile, knowing this is all yours.
90. **Make eye contact across a crowded room.** If you are out at a party or other social event, you can create a special moment by seeking out your partner across the room. Make eye contact, give a wink, and let them know you like what you see!
91. **Share together.** When you are with family or friends, share important news with them together. Are you going to have a baby? Are you leaving on a big trip, or starting a new business adventure? Share the news and excitement together.

The Little Things

> *"Enjoy the little things,*
> *for one day you may look back*
> *and realize they were the big things.*
> Robert Brault

It is the simple things in life that brings us together and keeps us connected...

92. **Bring them a little something, just because.** It doesn't have to be anything fancy, elaborate, or expensive, just something you know they will like and put it under their pillow, or a place where they will be the one to find it.

93. **Appreciate the little things they say and do.** The laundry is done, the lawn is mowed, the garbage is out, the kids are fed, and homework has been completed with a minimum of complaint. Even the day-to-day routine and normal things that make up a day well lived deserves some attention. Tell them how much you appreciate them for it.

94. **Ask about their day.** Caring about your partner by asking about their day is an intimate gesture and will be very appreciated. A word of caution: Don't insist on an answer or probe incessantly when they have obviously had a bad day or they need to process things before talking. They will talk when they're ready. This might be a better time for "Cave

Time," or "Run Her a Bubble Bath," both noted earlier.

95. **Go over your calendars together.** Take a few minutes each week to go over your calendars and understand what is going on in each other's lives. Sure, going over the family calendar is a good thing to avoid squabbles and mishaps about who picks up the kids or the dry cleaning, but the few moments taken to connect during this time can be made into an intimate moment by connecting with your partner, laughing as you propose and counter who needs to do what, and keeping it light. Be creative - and don't forget to schedule date night!

96. **Turn off the electronic devices.** Turn off the TV, the radio, the computer, ditch the cell phone, and *back away* from the video games. Disconnect from electronic distractions and reconnect with your partner. You could simply pretend the power is out, and play a game of your own! Strip poker by candlelight, anyone? Hmmm, the ideas are limitless!

97. **Read together.** Just you and your partner, a good light, and a cup of tea or coffee. Just sit and read one book out loud together, or reading your own book separately, it doesn't matter. Connect through the shared activity. Every now and then, reach out and touch just to let them know you're there.

98. **Take a trip to the "toy store."** This one can go one of three ways. His toy store might be the hardware or sports store, and hers might be the local craft store, or vice versa! It doesn't matter, sharing their passion, if even for a moment, is what is important to your partner. But the one we like the best is taking a trip to the *adult* entertainment store! Visit your local adult store together and whisper and giggle about all the gadgets and gizmos available for intimate adult pleasure. Buy something and explore! You know you want to!

99. **A gift certificate of time.** Give your partner a gift of an hour or two of your time. Your time is theirs for whatever they want or need. Yes, this could involve some "risk," but that is half the fun of this gift!

100. **A gift certificate for "Passion, Your Way."** Along a similar vein, give the gift of passion. It's all about them, for them, their needs, their desires, in any way they want!

101. **Exercise together.** Jog, go to the gym, get a motion-sensor game console and use it, or take yoga together. (By the way, guys, yoga IS a workout - REALLY - and good for you, so get over it already!) Learn a new sport together. The couple that sweats together - stays together! Right? OK, maybe that's taking it a bit too far – but at least you will be healthier for it. If you don't like working out together, intimate moments can still be created by taking a few seconds to connect before or after

hitting the gym. Let your partner know how much you appreciate them taking care of themselves in this way... and then notice, mention and touch the results from their effort!

102. **Play a game.** Play cards or a board game and maybe even play a video game together. As a couple, with family or friends, it doesn't matter. Intimacy can happen anywhere, anytime – in the open, or secretly. That's up to you!

103. **Take a class.** Take a cooking class, an art class, or a fly fishing class together. Or take separate classes to pursue your own interests and share with each other how much you enjoyed it and why.

104. **And last but not least – Dance together!** Whether you dance in the kitchen or take ballroom classes together, whether you consider yourself "clueless" or a wanna-be *Dancing With the Stars* pro, moving together in unison is one of the most intimate activities a couple can do together. And guys, partner dancing is the last great bastion of male dominance... You get to lead! Enjoy!

Putting it All Together

> *"Our intention creates our reality."*
> Wayne Dyer

Regardless of where your relationship is today, making changes, even the small, positive and simple changes we are suggesting here, may be challenging for one or both of you.

There is an expression we like to use, *"Change is easy, **thinking** about change is hard."* We discovered this expression in the book, *The Hundred Year Lifestyle*, by Dr. Eric Plasker, and we've been using it ever since! When you break down change to its simplest form, it is all about making a decision, the one decision in front of you, right now. If you and your partner have clarity of direction in your desire to create a loving relationship together, then making the "right" decision is easy. The challenge, and often times the overwhelming feelings of fear, come from **thinking** about all the things you may have to do, or all the time and effort it may take to reach an objective in order to affect change. But once a decision is made, actual change is the easy part... it can only be done step-by-step, one moment at a time, one decision at a time. Everyone can handle one step at a time so, in the end, change is easy!

To assist you in creating intimacy in your relationship and to help you get the most out of the simple concepts in this book, we suggest these basic steps:

1. *Create intention* with a written commitment to one another. A spoken and written commitment to your partner to provide intimacy in the way they need it. Commit to one another that you will respect your partner's needs for intimacy, whatever they may be, and allow them to be who they are, not what you wish them to be.

2. *Become attentive* by first understanding your own needs for intimacy, as well as your own communication style and natural way of being motivated, and sharing these things with your partner. Discuss what this means to you and how each can support the other in a way that is most meaningful to you and your partner.

   As we have discussed, to help you discover and understand your needs for intimacy as well as your partner's, we suggest going through the exercises we developed as well as reading through the 104 practical ideas provided and determine which ones resonate with you most. Better yet, review and discuss them with your partner as an opportunity to create an intimate moment.

3. **Practice using the Intimate Moment Cycle™** and, most importantly, have fun with it. No matter how intent you are or how attentive you and your partner try to be, you will likely miss a few opportunities. Stay positive, stay committed, laugh it off, and try-try again. If your partner misses an intimate gesture, simple say something like, *"Hey beautiful, intimate moment bulls-eye, right here,"* and point to your lips. Or some other fun expression. Always remember your commitment to one another and your intention to be intimate. The commitment isn't to be perfect, so embrace the miss-steps with a sense of humor and turn THAT time into an intimate moment by laughing together.

4. And finally, **continue to seek guidance** in each other and through other sources and resources. No one comes with an Operations Manual, and even if we did, things change over time.

    We also invite you to experience our website, www.TheCouplesGrowthChallenge.com, where you will find additional tools and resources that will continue to challenge you. Join the conversation in our interactive blog to ask questions and find solutions. You can even join our email mailing list to receive new and innovative ideas, such as **Passionate Pursuits**™ opportunities, and other tools designed for both men and women to help you grow and create the relationship of your dreams.

As an added treat, we've included our first **Passionate Pursuit**™ below. A Passionate Pursuit™ is a story or a scenario you read together for inspiration to help you create special moments together, or you can choose to reenact them to add a little fun and spice to your relationship. Each Passionate Pursuit™ gives you the idea and the framework to try something new, to escape "the day-to-day" for a time and explore each other in a different way, to learn something you didn't know before about your partner, and to help you rediscover the energy and vitality in your relationship, and so much more.

Remember our example Couple #3, Bob and Sarah, used earlier in the book? They are married with children. They know they love each other, and they love their kids. Over the years, however, their life has become ridiculously busy and very routine. They each feel disconnected and they both want the intimacy, romance and passion back in their relationship but they don't know where to begin to find what they've lost. We're going to use them to help us introduce you to **Passionate Pursuits**™.

An Introduction to Passionate Pursuits™

Let's look in on Bob and Sarah...

Bob looked up as Sarah walked across the lawn toward him. He saw a look in her eye that meant business, and he thought it best to stand to meet this head on. Taking a break from fixing the lawnmower, Bob wiped the grease from his hands as Sarah approached and he searched her eyes for a clue to what was on her mind. "Bob, we need to talk..."

Bob exhaled slowly before he spoke, "This I gathered... What's up, hon?"

"I'm not sure how to broach this subject, so bear with me, OK?"

"OK," Bob said as he braced himself for bad news.

"I miss us. Don't get me wrong. I love you. I love our children, and I love our life with our kids. I just miss **US**. Does that make sense?"

"Yeah, I think I know what you mean," Bob said with a sigh of relief. "I've been missing us also. I feel like life is going by like a blur, and we're so wrapped up in the kids and their activities, and work and board meetings... the lawn mower," as he waves a hand at it and shrugs, "that there isn't any time left for just us."

"Exactly! You're feeling that way too?," Sarah said as she sunk down to the grass, cross legged, and put her head in her hands.

Bob sat down next to her, put his arm around her, and pulled her close. "I love you, you know."

"I know, and I love you too, but I wonder if we're still IN love with each other anymore, you know? I feel so far away from you lately when we used to feel so close. We bicker a lot about nothing, really; and when we do talk, we don't seem to talk about anything anymore but work, kids, and who we think is going to be voted off tonight on "*Idol*." Sometimes we finish an entire meal without saying more than four sentences to each other, and we both fall into bed at night, too tired to do anything but sleep. I'm worried that won't sustain our relationship and I'm scared we're growing apart. I don't want our marriage to end in divorce."

Bob's posture improved immediately as he sat up ramrod straight with Sarah's last comment. "What do you mean, divorce? Are you thinking about a divorce, Sarah?"

"NO, that's not what I said, and it's not what I meant either. I don't want us to end in divorce because we've grown apart, because we don't know each other anymore. I want to change this now so we grow closer together, not farther apart with each anniversary."

"Well, that's what I want too," Bob said, "I want things to be more like it used to be for us. I know I haven't been very good at planning date nights, but I'm willing to make a commitment to do that for us."

"Well, I haven't been very good about doing that either; and it's not just up to you to plan things for us to do. I own half of that responsibility too, you know. But I did hear about something that I want us to try together."

"Really? Uh... What is it?" Bob sounded worried.

Sarah smiled, "You look scared! It's nothing too crazy, but I think it might help us find our way back to each other."

"I admit... I'm a little nervous."

"Me too, but I think I want to give this a try."

"I'm all ears..."

"Tammy at work told me about this and it sounds interesting. She said her husband wasn't sure about it either at first, but they had so much fun by the end of the evening they planned to do it again. Now, they do it all the time!"

"OK, you've REALLY got my attention now... What is it?"

"Promise you won't laugh?"

"No, but OK... I promise..."

"It's called Passionate Pursuits™."

Bob had to stop himself from chuckling, "Passion what?" He looked around to make sure the kids weren't within earshot, and dropped the volume of his voice before asking, "Is this some sex adventure thing or something?"

"Well, no, but we could take it there if we wanted to..."

Bob's eyes got big, "What? Really?"

Sarah laughed, "Yes – but seriously, are you listening?"

"Absolutely, I'm listening, with both ears! Let's hear it!"

"OK, OK..." Sarah smiled, "This may sound a little strange, but I really would like to try it."

"Alright, I'm game. Now, what IS it?"

"It's a scenario."

"A what?" Bob scrunched up his face and he looked puzzled.

"A scenario, or it could be a story."

"Uh... that's it?" Bob said, a little deflated.

"Well, yes. You read this short story together, or it could simply be a scenario that's presented, and then together you reenact it following some guidelines the authors provide. The stories give couples ideas to help them rediscover each other in their relationship."

"Sounds, uh… *interesting*…" Bob looked unconvinced.

"Are you still game?" Sarah questioned.

"Although I'm still a bit nervous and I'm certainly skeptical, I'm still game."

"Cool! I've made arrangements with a babysitter this Friday night. Look for an email from me later this week. Don't plan anything that evening. You're MINE from 6 o'clock on!" And with that, Sarah jumped up, kissed the top of Bob's head and turned toward the house.

"Wait a second! I still don't really know what this is all about!"

"Oh, you will. Trust me…" Sarah said with a sheepish grin, and for the first time in a long time, she felt a twinge of excitement in her belly that reminded her of how she felt years ago when they first started dating.

Bob stood up and scratched his head as he watched Sarah walk away with a bounce in her step she didn't have before, and he had a smile on his face as well.

A few days later, Sarah sent Bob an email that read…

> From: sarah123@email.com
> To: bob123@email.com
> Subject: Friday Night
>
> Hi, honey,
>
> As promised, please read the attached "Passionate Pursuit™" and bring your "A" game to the Starlight Lounge downtown this Friday night at 6:15 pm, dressed to impress!
>
> I'm really looking forward to this!
>
> Love you,
> Sarah

Attached to the email was the following...

Passionate Pursuit #1
Meeting for the First Time

The Purpose: The purpose of this pursuit is to (re-)discover your partner and to (re-)introduce yourself to them by pretending to meet your partner as if you were meeting for the very first time, **as you are today**.

The Set Up: To set-up this scenario, agree to meet at a location of your choice (a hotel lounge, a bar, a coffee shop…) at a time that works for both of you, but one partner should arrive 15 minutes before the other to secure a seat or table alone, where they can be easily "seen." This partner is the "pursued." The partner who arrives later is the "pursuer." Individually, each of you is planning an evening out. You are single and available, so take the time to dress to impress and take care in your appearance.

The Rules: The rules for this pursuit are as follows:

1. The location should be "neutral ground" and not familiar to either of you or where you would expect to run into friends, co-workers or family who know you as a couple.

2. The location should not be your home.

3. Except for emergencies, your cell phones are set to silent and you will accept no interruptions.

4. No "real life" discussions (as a married couple) are allowed. No discussions about your schedules, problems with kids, chores, etc., except in the context of the pursuit. As an example, you can mention that you have children, but remember the other person doesn't know anything about them. So ask questions about "each other's children," or your work, special interests, etc. You will be amazed about what you discover!

The Pursuit: You are to pretend that you do not know each other and that you are single and hopeful of meeting someone new tonight. In all other ways, however, you will be yourself and who you are today. You are not pretending to be someone else or who you were when you first met. You have the life you have now; with kids, work, interests, hobbies, friends and family. You are simply pretending that the other person knows NOTHING about those things and that you know nothing about their life.

When the "pursuer" arrives, look around the room and find a table or seat where you can catch the eye of the "pursued." Settle in, have a drink and relax for a few minutes. Let the anticipation build. Catch the eye of the pursued and make it known they have caught your attention. When you notice the pursued's glass getting low, approach, introduce yourself, ask to buy the next round, and ask to join them.

From here, for both the pursuer and the pursued, it is all about asking questions and actively listening. Who are they? What do they do? What are their hobbies, passions, desires, dreams, and needs? As the pursued, you find the pursuer fascinating and it is exciting to see someone take such interest in you. Remember, the pursuer knows nothing about you, so provide details, be open in your responses and ask questions and actively listen in return.

When you find the pace slowing, ask the following question, *"What question haven't I asked you tonight that you really hoped I would?"* This allows the other to tell you something they may have wanted you to know but have never had the opportunity before. When it's time to end the evening, the pursuer can say something like, *"This has been great! May I see you again?"* and you can set a time and place to continue your discovery of each other. You may choose to leave separately or together, and if the feeling is right, continue the evening elsewhere.

Note: It is best not to set expectations on what is to happen when you get home. The focus of this pursuit is getting to know one another as if you knew nothing about your partner. Whatever this might lead to later should be considered a bonus, not the objective!

"Wow! OK, Sarah, you've got my attention! This could be fun!" Bob thought as he tried, unsuccessfully, to turn his attention back to his report.

Friday finally arrives and both Bob and Sarah have a spring to their step as they get ready for work. With a wink and a kiss, Bob's the first to leave the house, smiling all the way to work.

Sarah took the afternoon off and hurried home to get ready. The babysitter will arrive at 5, and she has a lot to do. She wants to be at the lounge at 6 to find a good table. She can't wait to wear the new red dress she bought that Bob hasn't seen, and the little lacey undergarments he hasn't seen either! She feels the tingles in her tummy, and it makes her smile.

Sarah, looking stunning in her red dress and heels, arrives at the lounge glowing with excitement. She finds a little table in the corner that has a bit more privacy than the others, and she orders a glass of wine… and waits.

Bob was so excited all afternoon he could barely get through his meetings. At 5:15, he washed his face and shaved again to get rid of the 5 o'clock shadow, and he put on a crisp dress shirt. *"Well, here we go,"* he thought as he left his office.

Bob arrived at the lounge promptly at 6:15. Walking in, he looked around and saw a beautiful lady in a red dress, sitting alone. A bolt of electricity ran up his spine that he hadn't felt in a very long time. He made his way over to the bar and asked the bartender for a glass of Merlot. Bob stood at the bar a moment, sipping his wine and scanned the crowd again. Busy night, he thought. But his eyes were drawn back to the lady in red. Their eyes met. She smiled, as did he in return.

After a few minutes, Bob made his way over to her table, feeling excited. He is struck by how beautiful this woman is. He extends his hand, and she takes it, *"Hi, I'm Bob, may I buy you another drink?..."*

And so begins their *Passionate Pursuit!*

The next day, Bob meets a friend, at the gym to shoot hoops.

"You're in a good mood, what gives?" Adam says as he takes a shot.

"Well," Bob catches the basketball on the rebound and stops. "I met this incredible woman last night and I had the most amazing experience. Quite frankly, I'm still in awe about the entire evening."

"What?" Adam stopped his shot abruptly looking shocked. "Bob, are you having an affair?"

Bob replied with a grin, "Hmmm... I guess I am, and I'm loving every second of it!"

That same day, Sarah is talking with a girlfriend over coffee, "Tammy, you were right! I had the best time last night with Bob... It was such a fun, intimate evening! We really connected. Honestly, I think I'm falling in love with him all over again!"

"I told you so! That's great, Sarah!"

"I know! We talked and laughed all night! He told me things I never knew about him. I didn't know he listens to Aerosmith when he works out; or that he dreamed about being an astronaut when he was a boy and has always wanted to visit NASA and see a shuttle takeoff in person. I just assumed I knew everything about him already, having been married so long. I found out he's still the man I married, and much more. I even surprised him with a hotel room and we experienced Passionate Pursuit™ #2," she said a little sheepishly. "We really had a great time. Thank you for telling me about this!"

In Closing

We hope this little book, the first in our *LOVE from Strength*™ series, and our first Passionate Pursuit™ will help you rediscover, enhance and maintain the intimacy in your relationship so you can fuel the fires of romance and create a deeply passionate love affair that lasts a lifetime.

We would love to hear your story and how this process works for you in your relationship. We also value your feedback and invite you to connect with us by joining our mailing list through visiting our interactive website www.TheCouplesGrowthChallenge.com, where you will find an on-line community of support, additional Passionate Pursuits™ to experience, along with new ideas and information to enhance and grow your relationship.

We look forward to hearing from you.

Enjoy each other in love,

Wayne Ottum & Deborah Kiernan-Ottum

About the Authors

Wayne Ottum and Deborah Kiernan-Ottum are owners of Ottum Enterprises, LLC, a firm dedicated to helping people create the success they desire in their business, life and relationship through clarity of direction, purpose and values that leads to authentic and confident action, each and every day.

In 2003 Wayne founded Ottum Enterprises, LLC and began partnering with business owners to help them create a clear definition of success, to get focused, get real, and get moving, helping them to create *"a business plan with real meaning."* During this time, Wayne developed the firm's flagship coaching process, *The Business Growth Challenge*™. Through that process, Wayne discovered the synergy of using these successful business principles to help individuals create *"a business plan for life"* through *The Personal Growth Challenge*™ which is outlined in Wayne's book *"The POWER of living TODAY as a Business of ONE,"* (soon to be re-released as "LIVE from Strength.") Using these highly successful coaching processes, the firm has helped hundreds of business owners and individuals create the clarity needed to act confidently each day to reach the success they desire.

Wayne and Deborah have now taken these proven principles and processes and applied them to relationships to create *The Couples Growth Challenge*™ and the *LOVE from Strength*™ series of services. This coaching process helps couples clearly define the relationship they desire, understand their own needs for intimacy, romance and passion, along with the needs of their partner so that each of them can act confidently to give each other what they need so they can live the relationship of their dreams.

It should be noted that Wayne and Deborah do not claim to be relationship experts, therapists or counselors. They are, however, experts in helping people realize the power in **clarity**; clarity that leads to confident action toward your dreams and, ultimately, to the success you define. Such power comes from a clear direction, knowledge of your unique gifts, and a vision of success. This vision naturally compels you to act to achieve what you truly desire. By understanding your unique gifts and how you create real value, you can find real meaning and fulfillment in your life and relationships. A clearly defined set of values gives you the power to guide your daily decision-making. Knowledge is power and self-awareness is the most powerful knowledge of all! It is in this spirit that Wayne and Deborah have written *Create Intimacy... in as little as 8 seconds a day.*

If, however, your relationship is having serious issues beyond the reach of this little book, the authors encourage you to seek professional guidance.

To find out more about Wayne and Deborah and the unique and powerful coaching processes provided by Ottum Enterprises, please visit any of the following websites:

- www.OttumEnterprises.com
- www.TheBusinessGrowthChallenge.com
- www.ThePersonalGrowthChallenge.com
- www.TheCouplesGrowthChallenge.com

You can find Wayne's book, *The POWER of Living TODAY as a Business of ONE*, (soon to be re-released as *LIVE from Strength*) through popular on-line booksellers, as well as on their interactive personal growth website, www.ThePersonalGrowthChallenge.com, where you can also find other informative articles by Wayne and Deborah. This book guides you as an individual, to take proven business success principles (clarity of vision, mission, and values) and apply them to your personal life in a step-by-step format, helping you create *"a business plan for life"* that is truly authentic to you. It provides a simple process for discovering your authentic self and introduces you to a way of living that gives you the POWER and confidence you need to live the life of your dreams, each and every day!

Preview an excerpt from this powerful, groundbreaking book or purchase your copy today at: www.ThePersonalGrowthChallenge.com.

www.ingramcontent.com/pod-product-compliance
Lightning Source LLC
Chambersburg PA
CBHW061654040426
42446CB00010B/1733